# EAP Foundation: Academic Presentations

Sheldon Smith

# EAP Foundation: Academic Presentations

EAP Foundation: Academic Presentations
Copyright © 2018 Sheldon C.H. Smith

All rights reserved. No part of this publication may be reproduced, stored in a retrieval system, or transmitted, in any form or in any means – by electronic, mechanical, photocopying, recording or otherwise – without prior written permission.

ISBN 978-1-912579-00-6

First Edition

This book is published by Evident Press. For more information on this title and others in the *EAP Foundation* series, visit www.evidentpress.com.


Acknowledgements
Academic collocations listed at the start of each unit are derived from the Academic Collocation List (ACL), developed by Kirsten Ackermann and Yu-Hua Chen using the Pearson International Corpus of Academic English (PICAE). The lists were generated using the online ACL highlighter of the EAPFoundation.com website. See: http://www.eapfoundation.com/vocab/academic/acl/highlighter/.

The textual data in Unit 4, Exercise 4 and *Appendix 4: Data for visual aids* are taken from the OpenStax resources provided by Rice University. Acknowledgements are given where those texts occur.

Other data in *Appendix 4* are from various open source data sets (U.S. Bureau of Economic Analysis, The World Bank, WHO, CIA The World Factbook). Acknowledgements are given alongside the data.

# About the EAP Foundation series

The *EAP Foundation* series is written for EFL students who are preparing for, or currently studying at, a Western university, including those on foundation or pre-sessional courses. In contrast to many English language textbooks, which offer fragments of information scattered around a series of exercises, books in the *EAP Foundation* series focus on presenting practical information in a straightforward and readable manner, with exercises coming at the end of each unit as a way to check understanding and deepen comprehension. This straightforward presentation of material makes the books ideal not only for classroom use, but for independent study or review after class. There are checklists for each unit, which serve to foster self reflection and peer feedback, which are important principles behind the *EAP Foundation* series of books. All books have additional resources which can be downloaded, including worksheets, copies of checklists, teaching tips, lesson plans and mp3 recordings (for books in the speaking and listening series). This is ideal for personal use (if you are a student) or classroom use (if you are a teacher). These resources are available free of charge, using the access code available in *Appendix 1: Accessing online resources*. A full answer key is provided at the end of the book, meaning there is no need for a separate teacher's manual.

# About the author

Sheldon Smith has been teaching English for Academic Purposes (EAP) since 2002, working in the UK, Indonesia and China. Since 2005 he has been working on pathway programmes which prepare EFL students for university study at Western universities, chiefly in the USA, UK and Australia. In addition to textbooks for academic English, he is the author of several novels and text books for Chinese language learning. He is the founder and chief developer of the EAPFoundation.com website. He currently resides in Guangzhou, Guangdong province, China.

EAP Foundation: Academic Presentations

# CONTENTS

## INTRODUCTION ............................................................. 7
- Features of the book ................................................................. 7
- Structure of the book ............................................................... 7
- Internal/external links ............................................................. 9
- Key to language phrases .......................................................... 9

## PART I: PREPARATION & PLANNING ......... 11

### Unit 1: Preparation & Planning ........................................ 13
- Overview ................................................................................. 14
- Audience (Who) ...................................................................... 14
- Purpose (Why) ........................................................................ 14
- Tone (How) ............................................................................. 15
- Venue (Where) ....................................................................... 16
- Timing (When) ....................................................................... 17
- Content (What) ...................................................................... 17
- Planning .................................................................................. 18
- Checklist ................................................................................. 19
- Exercises ................................................................................. 20

## PART II: CONTENT ................................................. 27

### Unit 2: Structure ................................................................ 29
- Overview ................................................................................. 30
- Introduction ........................................................................... 30
- Main body ............................................................................... 31
- Conclusion .............................................................................. 31
- Q&A ........................................................................................ 32
- Checklist ................................................................................. 33
- Exercises ................................................................................. 34

### Unit 3: Language ............................................................... 39
- Overview ................................................................................. 40

    Language for introductions .................................................................. 40
    Language for visual aids ...................................................................... 42
    Transition phrases ................................................................................ 42
    Other phrases ........................................................................................ 43
    Language for concluding ..................................................................... 44
    Language for Q&A ................................................................................ 45
    Checklist ................................................................................................. 46
    Exercises ................................................................................................ 47

## Unit 4: Visual Aids .................................................................. 53
    Overview ................................................................................................ 54
    Types of visual aid ................................................................................ 54
    What to present in visual aids ............................................................ 56
    Guidelines for visuals ........................................................................... 57
    Referring to visuals .............................................................................. 58
    Checklist ................................................................................................. 58
    Exercises ................................................................................................ 59

# PART III: PERFORMANCE ....................... 65

## Unit 5: Body Language ............................................................ 67
    Overview ................................................................................................ 68
    Position .................................................................................................. 68
    Posture .................................................................................................. 69
    Movement ............................................................................................. 69
    Eye contact ........................................................................................... 70
    Checklist ................................................................................................. 71
    Exercises ................................................................................................ 72

## Unit 6: Delivery ........................................................................ 75
    Overview ................................................................................................ 76
    Pace ....................................................................................................... 76
    Pronunciation ....................................................................................... 76
    Volume .................................................................................................. 77
    Emphasis ............................................................................................... 77
    Checklist ................................................................................................. 78
    Exercises ................................................................................................ 79

**EAP Foundation: Academic Presentations**

# Appendices ........................................................... 83

**Appendix 1: Accessing online resources ........................................... 84**
   About online resources ............................................................. 84
   How to access online resources .................................................. 84

**Appendix 2: Answers to exercises ..................................................... 85**
   Unit 1 ........................................................................................ 85
   Unit 2 ........................................................................................ 89
   Unit 3 ........................................................................................ 93
   Unit 4 ........................................................................................ 96
   Unit 5 ........................................................................................ 99
   Unit 6 ...................................................................................... 101

**Appendix 3: Presentation topics .................................................... 103**
   Topic 1: Economics ................................................................. 103
   Topic 2: Health ....................................................................... 104
   Topic 3: Sociology .................................................................. 105

**Appendix 4: Data for visual aids ..................................................... 106**
   Economics data ....................................................................... 106
   Health data ............................................................................. 108
   Sociology data ........................................................................ 110

**Appendix 5: Presentation planning grid ......................................... 112**

**Appendix 6: Presentation outline .................................................. 114**

# Introduction

Presentations are a common part of academic life. Although giving a presentation can seem daunting at first, it is actually quite a routine task. Presentations all have the same basic structure and use similar signpost language. As long as you plan carefully and allow enough time to not only prepare the content but also practise to improve performance, you will be able to give an effective presentation time after time.

## Features of the book

As with all books in the *EAP Foundation* series, the units focus on presenting practical information in a straightforward and readable manner. There are additional tips in each unit to help you perform well. There are also numerous 'In short' boxes which give a summary of the main points covered (an example of one of these is given to the right). These will help you to preview the unit before reading in detail, and provide a useful way to review the unit later. Each unit also contains a checklist, which is used either to check understanding or to give feedback (to yourself or a peer). Each unit concludes with a range of exercises to check comprehension and deepen your understanding. At the end of the book there are appendices, giving information on accessing online resources, answers to exercises, three presentation topics, data for visual aids, a presentation planning grid and a presentation outline.

> **In short**
> The book has the following features:
> - Practical information
> - Additional tips
> - 'In short' summaries
> - Checklists
> - Exercises
> - Additional resources at the end of the book

## Structure of the book

The book begins by identifying questions to consider when preparing for your presentation, covering *audience*, *purpose*, *tone*, *venue*, *timing* and *content*. Planning is also considered in the first unit (*Unit 1: Preparation & Planning*). The book continues by examining presentation structure – *introduction*, *main body*, *conclusion* and *Q&A* – and considering what each section should contain (*Unit 2: Structure*). A key area which supports the structure, namely signpost language, is considered in a separate unit (*Unit 3: Language*), while an area which supports the content, namely visuals, is also

# EAP Foundation: Academic Presentations

considered separately (*Unit 4: Visual Aids*). The final areas of the book relate to presentation performance, namely body language (*Unit 5: Body Language*) and delivery (*Unit 6: Delivery*).

The following graphic summarises the structure of the book.

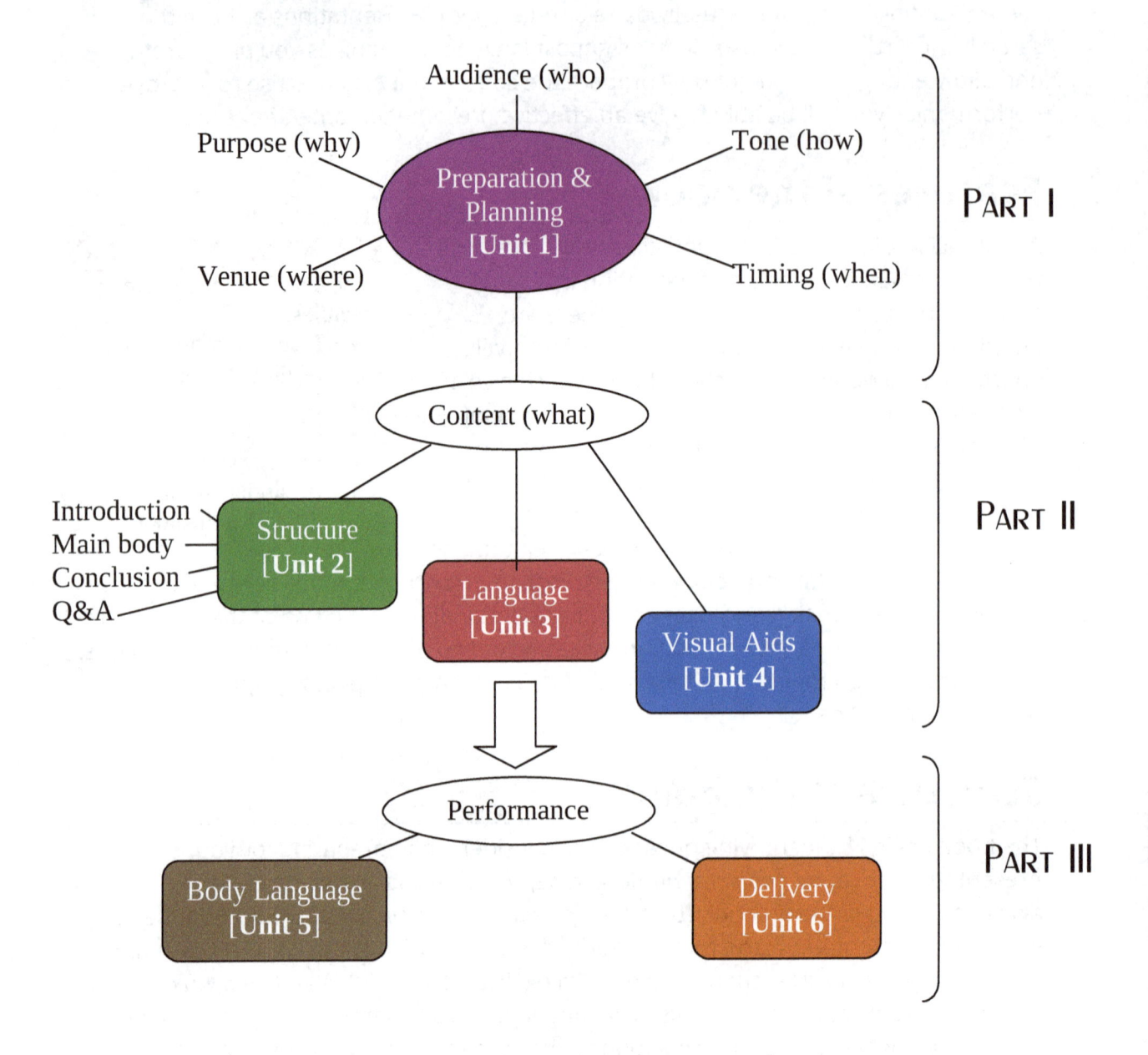

**Part I**
- Preparation & Planning [Unit 1]
  - Audience (who)
  - Purpose (why)
  - Tone (how)
  - Venue (where)
  - Timing (when)

**Part II**
- Content (what)
  - Structure [Unit 2]: Introduction, Main body, Conclusion, Q&A
  - Language [Unit 3]
  - Visual Aids [Unit 4]

**Part III**
- Performance
  - Body Language [Unit 5]
  - Delivery [Unit 6]

# Internal/external links

Some internal links have been included in the book. These will point you backwards or forwards to other units which are related to the area under discussion, which will help you make connections between different aspects of giving a presentation. The following is an example of an internal link to an *earlier* section of the book. Note the arrows pointing *backwards* (i.e. to the left).

⏪ *See* Venue *in* Unit 1: Preparation and Planning *for questions about the venue, including rearranging the furniture before your talk.*

The following is an example of an internal link to a *later* section of the book. Note the arrows pointing *forwards* (i.e. to the right).

*See* Unit 3: Language *for more examples of language to use in the Q&A section.* ⏩

Some content may be closely related to another aspect of EAP. For example, transitions in a presentation are very similar to transitions in lectures. In this case, there may be an external link to another book in the *EAP Foundation* series. The following is an example of an external link. Note the arrows pointing *forwards* and *backwards* (i.e. out of the book). The colouring is also different for clarity (dark background with white lettering).

⏪ *For more on how transition phrases are used in lectures, see* EAP Foundation: Academic Listening. ⏩

# Key to language phrases

In *Unit 3: Language* the language phrases are shown in a way which minimises space and shows how the parts of the phrase can be combined. For example:

- My | presentation / talk | will | take / last | about 20 minutes.

These parts can be combined into four possible sentences, as follows:
- My <u>presentation</u> will <u>take</u> about 20 minutes.
- My <u>presentation</u> will <u>last</u> about 20 minutes.
- My <u>talk</u> will <u>take</u> about 20 minutes.
- My <u>talk</u> will <u>last</u> about 20 minutes.

**EAP Foundation: Academic Presentations**

# Part I:
## Preparation & Planning

**EAP Foundation: Academic Presentations**

# Unit 1: Preparation & Planning

## Learning Outcomes

By the end of this unit, you should:
- understand the importance of preparation for giving a good presentation;
- know how to prepare for a presentation by considering six areas: audience, purpose, tone, venue, timing and content;
- be aware of key questions to ask regarding each of these six areas;
- understand the importance of planning in order to deliver an effective presentation;
- be aware of the different stages involved when planning a presentation.

By completing the exercises, you will also:
- understand some common problems encountered when giving presentations;
- be aware of actions you can take during the preparation stage to avoid these common problems;
- study examples of general and specific purpose;
- begin answering key preparation questions related to a presentation you will give;
- set deadlines for stages of work for a presentation you will give.

## Key Vocabulary

*Nouns*
- audience
- purpose
- tone
- venue
- timing
- content

*Verbs*
- prepare
- plan (*also a noun*)
- inform
- persuade
- instruct
- motivate
- entertain

*Adjectives*
- general
- specific
- informational
- persuasive
- instructional
- motivational
- entertaining

## Additional Vocabulary

*Academic Collocations*
- final section (adj + n)
- high score (adj + n)
- key elements (adj + n)
- logical arguments (adj + n)
- potential problems (adj + n)
- specific focus (adj + n)
- specific purpose (adj + n)
- technical problems (adj + n)
- give a presentation (v + n)
- present arguments (v + n)

*AWL words*
For AWL words in Unit 1, access the online resources (see *Appendix 1* for instructions).

# EAP Foundation: Academic Presentations

## Overview

Giving a presentation can be an incredibly daunting task. Speaking in public is many people's greatest fear. However, even apparently confident speakers may be extremely nervous before or during a talk. The reason they appear so confident is that they have spent enough time preparing. They therefore understand their topic well and know what they are going to talk about and how they are going to say it.

> **In short**
> When preparing your presentation, you should consider the following:
> - Who – audience
> - Why – purpose
> - How – tone
> - Where – venue
> - When – timing
> - What – content

Three key elements to consider during the preparation stage of any form of academic output, including presentations, are the audience, purpose and tone: the who, why and how. When preparing a presentation it is also important to consider the venue (where), the timing (when), and, most importantly, the content (what). Each of these is considered in more detail below.

Planning is also a key ingredient of success. Without good planning, too much preparation is done at the last minute, and the presentation will not be as effective. The stages involved in planning a presentation are considered in the final section of this unit.

## Audience (Who)

Who your audience is will determine what you say and how you say it. A group of professors who are specialists in your field is a very different audience from a group of first year students with little knowledge of the topic you are presenting on. The following are key questions to answer about the audience as you prepare your presentation.
- How many people will be in the audience?
- Who are they?
- What do they know about the topic?
- Why are they attending the presentation?

## Purpose (Why)

Why you are giving the presentation, in other words the purpose, may seem quite straightforward. Often you are giving the presentation because you have to, for example because it is a compulsory assignment on your course, and you may think your purpose is something along the lines of 'To get a high score!' However, this is the purpose of the presentation *in relation to you*.

# Unit 1: **Preparation & Planning**

What is more important is the purpose of the presentation *in relation to the audience*. You need to think about what they will gain by listening to your presentation, in other words what you want them to know, believe or do at the end that they did not already know, believe or do before your talk. This depends, of course, on who the audience is and what they already know about the topic (see *Audience* above). Being clear about your purpose will not only help the audience understand the main message, but will also ensure you select appropriate content (see *Content* below). This is similar to the way a thesis statement in writing helps both the reader to follow the text, and the writer to know what to include.

Your presentation will have a *specific* purpose, which depends on the topic and focus and your approach to the task, and you will usually tell the audience this at the start of your talk. While there are countless possibilities for the specific purpose, all of them can be categorised as one of five types of *general* purpose.

> **Types of purpose**
> The following are types of general purpose your presentation may have:
> - To inform
> - To persuade
> - To instruct
> - To motivate
> - To entertain

- **To inform**. An informational presentation seeks to give or report information.
- **To persuade**. Persuasive presentations seek to present arguments to convince the audience regarding a particular point of view.
- **To instruct**. Instructive presentations seek to instruct or 'educate' the audience on a particular topic.
- **To motivate**. Motivational presentations seek to arouse interest in a topic, and may encourage the audience to take action. This type of presentation is common in the business field, though less common in academic settings.
- **To entertain**. An entertaining presentation seeks to present material in a humorous way. It is possibly the least academic and most difficult to deliver.

Key questions for purpose are:
- What is the *general* purpose of your presentation (*to inform*, *to persuade*, etc.)?
- What is the *specific* purpose of your presentation?
- What will the audience gain by listening to your presentation?

# Tone (How)

The tone of your presentation comes from your attitude towards the topic and how you convey this to the audience. It can range from serious to humorous to emotional, and as with any kind of spoken or written output, it will largely depend on the audience and purpose. Just as an academic report is different in tone from a letter to a friend, so a formal presentation to a large group of academics will be different in tone from an informal presentation to a small group of fellow students.

# EAP Foundation: Academic Presentations

In writing, the tone depends mainly on the language, in other words the vocabulary and grammar. Language is likewise important for setting the tone of an academic presentation. In general, most academic presentations will be fairly formal, though not as formal as written academic English, meaning there will be more shorter sentences, simpler grammatical structures, more use of active rather than passive, and more informal words such as 'So' and 'And' and 'But' instead of 'As a result' and 'In addition' and 'However'.

There are, however, two additional aspects of tone in a presentation which are not found in writing. One of these is your *presence*. This means your voice and body – how you sound and how you look. How you dress will play a part: smart clothes signal a serious presentation, while T-shirt and jeans suggest something very casual. Another aspect of a presentation which is different from writing and which adds to the tone is the images you use. Usually there will be more images than in writing, possibly including video clips.

Key questions to consider in relation to tone are:
- What tone do you want to convey to the audience (serious, humorous, etc.)?
- How will you convey this using your language, voice and body?
- What do you plan to wear? Does this match your intended tone?
- What images or video do you plan to use? Do these match your intended tone?

# Venue (Where)

Where you give your presentation is also going to be important. Presenting in a small room, with a maximum capacity of 20 people, is very different from presenting in a large auditorium which can hold hundreds of people. Even if the size of the audience is the same for both, other factors are different, such as the sound and how loudly you have to speak.

Some important questions relating to venue are:
- How big is the room?
- How easy will it be for the audience to see/hear you?
- What equipment is available, e.g. projector, computer, speakers, microphone, whiteboard?
- Can you use your own equipment, e.g. laptop?
- If you are using someone else's computer, what software is available?
- Is it possible to access the room before the presentation, to practise or to get set up?
- What furniture is in the room (chairs, desks, etc.)?
- Can you rearrange the furniture before your presentation?

> **Presentation Tip: Back up!**
> Many good presentations have been ruined by technical problems, e.g. broken computers, corrupt memory sticks, or PPTs prepared on newer versions of Office. Don't let yours be one of them! Anticipate potential problems, and make sure you have a back-up plan in case things go wrong!

# Unit 1: **Preparation & Planning**

## Timing (When)

There are several aspects to consider in relation to timing. The most one is how long your presentation should be. The longer it is, the more you will be able to include. When you give your presentation is also crucial. You want to prepare your presentation in advance, so you need to make sure you have enough time (see *Planning* section below). The time of day may also important. If you are presenting just after lunch, for example, your audience may be sleepy, which may affect your approach and content.

Important questions about timing are:
- How long should the presentation be?
- When (what date) is the presentation?
- What time is the presentation?
- How much time do you have to get ready?

## Content (What)

The content of the presentation is the final area you should consider, as it depends on all of the above. For many presentations at university the topic will be given in advance, which will limit what you can include. However, you may still need to narrow the topic to a specific focus. A presentation will not be as in-depth as an essay or report and you will therefore have to decide what elements to include and which ones to omit.

Having a clear purpose (see *Purpose* above) is especially important in determining the content. If your general purpose is *to inform*, you will want to select the strongest information and data available. If your general purpose is *to persuade*, you will need to choose convincing and logical arguments and evidence. If you plan *to instruct*, you will need to research the topic thoroughly and may need to include quite a lot of detail. If your purpose is *to motivate*, you will need to choose interesting and inspiring stories and quotes and present them with vivid language. Finally, if your purpose is *to entertain*, you will need to find humorous stories to include, or some other way to amuse the audience.

Important questions about content are:
- What is the topic of your presentation?
- Do you need to narrow the topic?
- Do you need to do any reading/research?
- What areas will you include?
- What areas can you omit?
- Does the type of information you have chosen match your purpose?

# EAP Foundation: Academic Presentations

# Planning

As mentioned at the start of the unit, it is not enough simply to prepare for a presentation; you must ensure you allow enough time to prepare *well*. Planning will help you to achieve this.

Planning means making a step-by-step guide to achieve your purpose, in this case, to deliver an effective presentation. To make your plan you will therefore need to understand the different steps involved. The first step, as with any kind of academic output, will be to understand the task and what you need to do. Ask other students or your tutor if you are not sure. After this, you need to prepare by considering the areas above, namely audience, purpose, tone, venue, timing and content. The content will be the most difficult area, and in order to decide what to include you will probably need to research the topic in more depth. The content will probably be supported by some kind of visual aid, and the next step will be to design this. Once you are fairly sure of the content and have some kind of visual, you can begin to practise the presentation. If possible, you should try to get feedback – from peers, your tutor or yourself – and use this to make improvements to the content and performance. Don't forget to practise answering questions to help you prepare for the Q&A section. Further practice, feedback and improvement may be useful. At this point, you should be almost ready to give the presentation, and will be making final arrangements such as finishing your PowerPoint, copying any handouts, and checking the venue. It will then be time to give your presentation. Your task should not end there though as you will want to get feedback on your performance in order to reflect and improve next time.

| **In short** |
|---|
| When planning your presentation, you need to: |
| • Understand the task |
| • Prepare for the task |
| • Research the topic |
| • Select content |
| • Make visual aids |
| • Practise |
| • Make improvements, based on feedback |
| • Continue practice |
| • Make final improvements |
| • Make final arrangements (finish PPT, copy handouts, check venue) |
| • Give presentation |
| • Reflect on performance |

# Unit 1: Preparation & Planning

## Checklist

Below is a checklist for preparation and planning. Use it to check your understanding of the main points of this unit.

| Item | OK? | Comments |
|---|---|---|
| I understand the importance of preparation and planning for a good presentation. | | |
| I know the six different areas I need to consider when preparing. | | |
| I know key questions related to *audience*. | | |
| I know different types of *general purpose* (e.g. *to inform*). | | |
| I know key questions related to *purpose*. | | |
| I understand the elements which make up the *tone* of an academic presentation. | | |
| I know key questions related to *tone*. | | |
| I know key questions related to *venue*. | | |
| I know key questions related to *timing*. | | |
| I understand how *content* relates to *purpose*. | | |
| I know key questions related to *content*. | | |
| I know the stages to consider when planning my presentation. | | |

# EAP Foundation: Academic Presentations

# Exercises

## Exercise 1: **Comprehension**

Answer the following questions about this unit. Either do this after reading the unit, or make notes first then use your notes to answer the questions.

1. What are the six key areas to consider when preparing a presentation? Write them below, then match each one to the appropriate *wh-* question word. An example has been done.

   - audience – *who*
   - 
   - 
   - 
   - 
   - 

2. Write down *two* questions you can ask about the audience.
   - 
   - 

3. Why is the purpose 'To get a high score!' not an appropriate one?
   _____
   _____

4. The *general* purpose of a presentation is often expressed using a verb. Write down *five* such verbs.
   -                                    •
   -                                    •
   - 

5. Which of the purposes in question 4 above are most suited to *academic* presentations?

6. How is the tone of an academic presentation *similar to* academic writing? How is it *different*?
   _____
   _____
   _____
   _____

7. What is a 'back-up plan', and why is it important to have one for your presentation?
   _____
   _____

# Unit 1: **Preparation & Planning**

**8** Why might the time of day you give your presentation be important?

_____
_____

**9** How is the content of an *informational* presentation different from a *persuasive* one?

_____
_____
_____

**10** Complete the stages in *planning a presentation* by using words from the box to fill the gaps.

| Verbs | | Nouns |
|---|---|---|
| Continue | Understand | arrangements |
| Reflect | Practise | visual aids |
| Research | Give | improvements |
| Prepare | Select | improvements |

1. _____ the task
2. _____ for the task
3. _____ the topic
4. _____ content
5. Make _____
6. _____
7. Make _____
8. _____ to practise
9. Make final _____
10. Make final _____
11. _____ presentation
12. _____ on performance

# EAP Foundation: Academic Presentations

## Exercise 2: **Solving Common Problems**

Study the following problems which might be encountered when giving a presentation. All of them could have been solved by better preparation. For each problem:
- decide which of the six areas above it relates to;
- try to think of one or more solutions which could have been taken when *preparing*.

An example has been done for you.

| Problem | Area | Possible solution(s) – *when preparing* |
|---|---|---|
| 1. The projector in the room does not work. | Venue | - Prepare handouts for the audience.<br>- Be ready to give the presentation *without* PPT. |
| 2. The computer in the room has an older version of Microsoft Office and your PowerPoint does not display properly. | | |
| 3. The presentation is too technical and the audience cannot follow the main points. | | |
| 4. The audience grows bored with the presentation and at the end, someone asks what it was about. | | |
| 5. You have prepared a 30 minute presentation, but are told you can only talk for ten. | | |
| 6. You have prepared ten handouts for the audience, but when you get to the room you find there are 50 people. | | |
| 7. You prepared a ten minute presentation, but after fifteen minutes you are only halfway through and are told to stop. | | |
| 8. You try to make your presentation humorous by including several jokes, but no one laughs. | | |

# Unit 1: Preparation & Planning

## Exercise 3: General and Specific Purpose

This exercise will help you understand how *specific purpose* relates to *general purpose*.

**First**, complete the 'Type' column by entering the adjective form of the general purpose verb (e.g. the adjective of *to inform* is *informational*). Look back in the unit if you need to.

| Type | General Purpose |
| --- | --- |
| informational | to inform |
|  | to persuade |
|  | to instruct |
|  | to motivate |
|  | to entertain |

**Then**, identify which type of presentation each of the following 'Specific Purpose Examples' is for. An example has been done for you.

| Specific Purpose Examples | Type |
| --- | --- |
| a) The purpose of my presentation is to inform you of the different types of purpose a presentation can have. | informational |
| b) What I want to do today is show why informational presentations are better than instructional ones. |  |
| c) My purpose today is to outline simple ways you can exercise while at work, and, hopefully, get you exercising more! |  |
| d) My purpose this afternoon is to show you how to give a terrible presentation! |  |
| e) My purpose today is to report on how often Business students use persuasive presentations. |  |
| f) My purpose today is to demonstrate how to give an effective presentation. |  |
| g) I'm here today to introduce the findings of our research project on eating habits in the over-sixties. |  |
| h) What I'm going to do this morning is explain why global warming is the most significant threat to our planet today. |  |

**Finally**, make a note of the language which helped you to match the *specific purpose* to the *general purpose*.

# EAP Foundation: Academic Presentations

## Exercise 4: **Preparation**

The following are the questions in the unit above. Try to answer as many as you can. If you can't answer some yet (for example, you may not be sure about the content until later), highlight those questions, and be sure you can answer them before your presentation.

| Area | Questions | Answers |
|---|---|---|
| Audience | • How many people will be in the audience?<br><br>• Who are they?<br><br>• What do they know about the topic?<br><br>• Why are they attending the presentation? | |
| Purpose | • What is the *general* purpose of your presentation (*inform*, *persuade*, etc.)?<br><br>• What is the *specific* purpose?<br><br>• What will the audience gain by listening to your presentation? | |
| Tone | • What tone do you want to convey?<br><br>• How will you convey this using your language, voice and body?<br><br>• What do you plan to wear?<br><br>• What images/video do you plan to use? Do these match your intended tone? | |

# Unit 1: Preparation & Planning

## Exercise 4: Preparation (cont'd)

*Note: If you do not have a presentation to work on for Exercise 4 and Exercise 5, you can prepare one using one of the topics in* Appendix 3: Presentation topics.

| Area | Questions | Answers |
|---|---|---|
| Venue | • How big is the room?<br>• How easy will it be for the audience to see/hear you?<br>• What equipment is available, e.g. projector, computer, speakers, microphone, whiteboard?<br>• Can you use your own laptop?<br>• If you are using someone else's computer, what software is available?<br>• Is it possible to access the room before the presentation, to practise or set up?<br>• What furniture is in the room?<br>• Can you rearrange the furniture? | |
| Timing | • How long should the presentation be?<br>• When (what date) is the presentation?<br>• What time is the presentation?<br>• How much time do you have to get ready? | |
| Content | • What is the topic of your presentation?<br>• Do you need to narrow the topic?<br>• Do you need to do any reading/research?<br>• What areas will you include?<br>• What areas can you omit?<br>• Does the type of information you have chosen match your purpose? | |

**EAP Foundation: Academic Presentations**

## Exercise 5: **Planning your Presentation**

Complete the following planning chart for a presentation you will give. Under 'When?' try to put a range (e.g. 22 Nov-29 Nov) or the date when this will be finished (e.g. 29 Nov). Remember to come back later to check your progress (is this stage complete?) and consider whether you need to make any adjustments to your planned dates. [*Note: A copy of this table can be downloaded from the website. See* Appendix 1 *for instructions*.]

| Stage | When? | Progress |
|---|---|---|
| Understand presentation task and requirements. | | |
| Consider audience, purpose, tone, venue, timing and content. | | |
| Research the topic (if necessary) and make notes. | | |
| Select content for presentation. | | |
| Make visual aids (PPT, handouts). | | |
| Begin practising. | | |
| Make improvements (to content, performance) based on feedback. | | |
| Continue practising. | | |
| Make final improvements, based on further feedback. | | |
| Make final arrangements (finish PPT, copy handouts, check room). | | |
| Give presentation! | | |
| Receive feedback, reflect, seek ways to improve. | | |

# PART II:
## CONTENT

**EAP Foundation: Academic Presentations**

# Unit 2: **Structure**

## Learning Outcomes

By the end of this unit, you should:
- understand the typical structure of a presentation;
- understand the different functions of the introduction;
- be aware of different types of 'hook' to arouse the audience's interest;
- know what you should do in the main body of a presentation;
- understand what a good conclusion should contain;
- know what the Q&A section is and how to tackle it;
- be aware of different types of Q&A question.

By completing the exercises, you will also:
- identify parts of an introduction;
- identify content of a presentation;
- identify different types of Q&A question;
- practise giving your presentation and get feedback on *content*.

## Key Vocabulary

*Nouns*
- introduction
- main body
- conclusion
- Q&A
- hook
- clarification
- expansion
- challenge

*Adjectives*
- off-topic

*Phrases*
- arouse interest (v + n)
- rhetorical question (adj + n)

## Additional Vocabulary

*Academic Collocations*
- academic work (adj + n)
- brief summary (adj + n)
- main task (adj + n)
- particular focus (adj + n)
- vital part (adj + n)
- relatively straightforward (adv + adj)
- clearly defined (adv + past verb)
- directly related (adv + past verb)

**EAP Foundation: Academic Presentations**

# Overview

The general structure of a presentation is much like any other academic work, such as an essay or a lecture. It too has an introduction, a main body, and a conclusion. Unlike an essay or a lecture, it has a section which comes *afterwards*, namely the Q&A, which is when you will answer questions from the audience. Each area is discussed in this unit.

# Introduction

The introduction is a vital part of your presentation, as it sets the stage for the rest of your talk. The main task will be to explain the purpose and content of your talk, though there are several other 'housekeeping' tasks you need to achieve, such as greeting the audience and explaining when you will answer questions.

A presentation will often begin with a 'hook', in other words something which will arouse the audience's interest. This needs to be kept fairly short, possibly just one or two sentences. Although a hook is less important in an academic presentation than in other types of talk, such as a business presentation where the presenter needs to impress the client, it is still a useful device. If you can gain the audience's interest at the start, they are more likely to pay attention to your main points, and you are therefore more likely to achieve your aim. A hook is especially important if your presentation is *motivational* or *humorous*. There are several common types of hook for presentations, including a story, a video or graphic, or a rhetorical question which will be answered later in the presentation.

| In short |
|---|
| In the Introduction, you need to:<br>• arouse interest - ask a question, tell a story;<br>• greet the audience;<br>• introduce yourself;<br>• state the topic and focus;<br>• state the purpose;<br>• outline the structure - tell them what you are going to tell them;<br>• say how long the presentation will last;<br>• say when you will be answering questions (Q&A). |

| Types of hook |
|---|
| The following are types of hook for presentations:<br>• story;<br>• video/graphic;<br>• humorous anecdote;<br>• rhetorical question;<br>• interesting or controversial statement. |

After the hook, your introduction should continue with two 'housekeeping' items, namely greeting the audience and introducing yourself and any co-presenters (if it is a group presentation). After this you should tell the audience the topic (e.g. *global warming*), as well as your particular focus (e.g. *causes* of global warming). You should also inform the audience of what you hope to achieve in your presentation (your purpose), as well as explaining how the presentation will be organised (the structure). This should usually be

# Unit 2: **Structure**

backed up by a visual aid, such as a PowerPoint slide, which shows the structure of the talk. The introduction should conclude with two more 'housekeeping' items, namely saying how long your presentation will be, and when you will be answering questions.

## Main body

The main body presents the ideas and information which will achieve the purpose you stated in the introduction. You need to be selective about the material in order to keep to the time available, and should present the material in clearly defined sections. Most presentations, even very long ones, will have two to four main sections; more is possible, though it can difficult to follow all the arguments. You also need to make sure you maintain the audience's interest and understanding. Although this sounds difficult, it is relatively straightforward as long as the information is presented in a logical sequence, emphasising main points, and making the structure clear via signpost phrases. Visual aids will also be an important part of your main body, so plan these well.

> **Think 'essay'**
> A presentation is similar to an essay. In the introduction you will state the purpose and structure (similar to a *thesis statement*). The main body will have clear sections (similar to *paragraphs*), introduced using appropriate transition phrases (similar to *topic sentences*). *Logical ordering* of ideas is important. The conclusion, just as in an essay, will contain a *summary*.

> **In short**
> In the main body, you should:
> - present important data/material;
> - have clearly defined sections (usually two to four);
> - use signpost phrases to help the audience follow the ideas;
> - draw the audience's attention to important points;
> - use visual aids to reinforce the verbal message.

## Conclusion

The conclusion should provide a simple yet strong end to your presentation. As this is the final part, it is the part the audience is likely to remember most clearly. You need to summarise the main points, and link these to the purpose of your presentation to show how this has been achieved. You should emphasise what the audience has learnt, and what you want them to remember, ideally giving them a final 'take-away' message, which is the one main idea you want them to remember from your presentation. It is polite to close by thanking the audience for their time. Finally, you should invite questions from the audience (the Q&A session, considered next).

> **In short**
> In the conclusion, you should:
> - give a brief summary of the major points - tell them what you told them;
> - be sure to link the summary to the purpose of your presentation;
> - give a final 'take-away' message;
> - close (by thanking the audience);
> - invite questions (the Q&A).

# Q&A

At the end of the presentation you should answer questions from the audience. This is the Question and Answer or Q&A session. At this point your presentation becomes more interactive, as the one-way traffic of you talking to the audience becomes two-way as they ask you to clarify your points or give more information. The Q&A can be intimidating, as you do not know what questions your audience will ask. It is an often overlooked part, as students spend hours rehearsing their presentation but do not practise answering questions. You can help with this by anticipating questions as you prepare, and by making sure you thoroughly research your topic. It is important to make sure you understand the question; a good technique is to repeat or rephrase the question to check ('Do you mean...?'). If you really do not know the answer, say so, but inform the questioner that you will do more research and answer the question later. As a matter of courtesy, you should check that you have given a satisfactory answer ('Does that answer your question?').

> **In short**
> For the Q&A session, you should:
> - think of questions you might be asked as you prepare your talk;
> - make sure you understand the question – check if unsure;
> - don't be afraid to say you don't know, but make it clear you will answer later;
> - check that your answer is satisfactory.

Although there is an almost endless list of questions you could be asked at the end of your presentation, all of them can be classified as one of four types.

- **Clarification**. The questioner did not understand. You should repeat or rephrase the information, adding detail as necessary.
- **Expansion**. The questioner wants more information. You should make sure you research widely and know your topic well
- **Challenge**. The questioner has a different opinion or interpretation. You should consider all sides of the argument as you prepare to help you tackle this type of question.
- **Off-topic**. The question is not related to the topic. It is best to politely refuse to answer (e.g. 'That's an interesting question, but not directly related to what I've talked about. Maybe we can discuss that later.').

> **Presentation Tip: Do your research!**
> Although a presentation has less content than a report or essay, you should still read widely on the topic, as this will not only allow you to select the most suitable information, but also help you tackle the Q&A.

> *See* Unit 3: Language *for more examples of language to use in the Q&A section.* ▶▶

Unit 2: **Structure**

# Checklist

Below is a checklist for structure. Use it to help you prepare, or ask a peer to use it to assess you when you practise.

| Item | OK? | Comments |
|---|---|---|
| In the introduction, the speaker:<br>• arouses interest – question, story;<br>• greets the audience;<br>• introduces him/herself;<br>• states the topic and focus;<br>• states the purpose;<br>• gives the structure;<br>• gives the timing;<br>• mentions the Q&A. | | |
| In the main body, the speaker:<br>• selectively presents important data;<br>• has clear sections;<br>• comments on important information;<br>• uses visual aids. | | |
| In the conclusion, the speaker:<br>• reviews the purpose;<br>• summarises the main points;<br>• gives a final 'take-away' message;<br>• invites questions. | | |
| In the Q&A section, the speaker:<br>• answers all questions;<br>• repeats questions if (s)he is unsure what the questioner asked;<br>• says (s)he will answer the question later if (s)he does not know the answer;<br>• checks that each answer is satisfactory. | | |

# EAP Foundation: Academic Presentations

# Exercises

## Exercise 1: Comprehension

Answer the following questions about this unit. Either do this after reading the unit, or make notes first then use your notes to answer the questions.

1 Put the following parts of a presentation Introduction into the order they *usually* occur. An example has been done for you.

give structure    greet audience    give timing    state topic and focus
~~arouse interest~~    state purpose    introduce yourself    give information about Q&A

    a) arouse interest                 e)
    b)                                f)
    c)                                g)
    d)                                h)

2 What is a 'hook' and why might it be best to start with this?

3 Give three different types of 'hook' which can be used in presentations.
- 
- 
- 

4 Some writers describe the outline of a presentation in this way: *Tell them what you are going to tell them; tell them; then tell them what you told them.* What do you think this means? Why might it be good advice?

5 What are the elements of an effective conclusion?

# Unit 2: Structure

6 What is a 'take-away' message and why is it important?
_____
_____

7 In what way is the Q&A different from the rest of the presentation?
_____
_____

8 What are the four different types of Q&A question given in this unit?
- 
- 
- 
- 

## Exercise 2: Identifying Parts of an Introduction

Study the following introduction to a presentation. Identify the different stages. An example has been done for you.

Let me begin by asking you a question: How do you prefer to learn? Perhaps you prefer to be in a group, or perhaps you study better on your own. Perhaps you learn best by listening, or perhaps you remember information better if you see it. Maybe you like to snack while you learn, have music on, and so on and so forth. These differences in the way we like to learn are called learning styles, and understanding your own preferences can be an important first step in improving how you study. **Good afternoon everyone.** I'm Steven Kirby, from the department of Educational Psychology, and what I want to look at today is learning styles, focusing on two of the main models of learning style used in educational contexts. I'll begin by giving a historical overview of learning styles, then give details about the two main models, namely the VAK model and the Dunn and Dunn model. I'll conclude by considering how learning styles can improve study. My aim today is to get you thinking about your own learning style and how you can use it to improve your learning. My presentation should last around twelve minutes. You may have some questions as we go along, but I'd be grateful if you could wait until the end of my presentation before you ask them.

- arouse interest
- greet the audience
- introduce yourself
- state the topic and focus
- state the purpose
- outline the structure
- say how long the presentation will last
- say when you will answer questions

**EAP Foundation: Academic Presentations**

## Exercise 3: **Identifying Content of a Presentation**

Study the introduction to a presentation in Exercise 2 again. Identify the *topic and focus* as well as the *specific purpose*, and record them in the mind map below. Remember that the *topic* is a noun, while the *purpose* is a verb. Then identify the *main idea* of each of the three sections, and record this information.

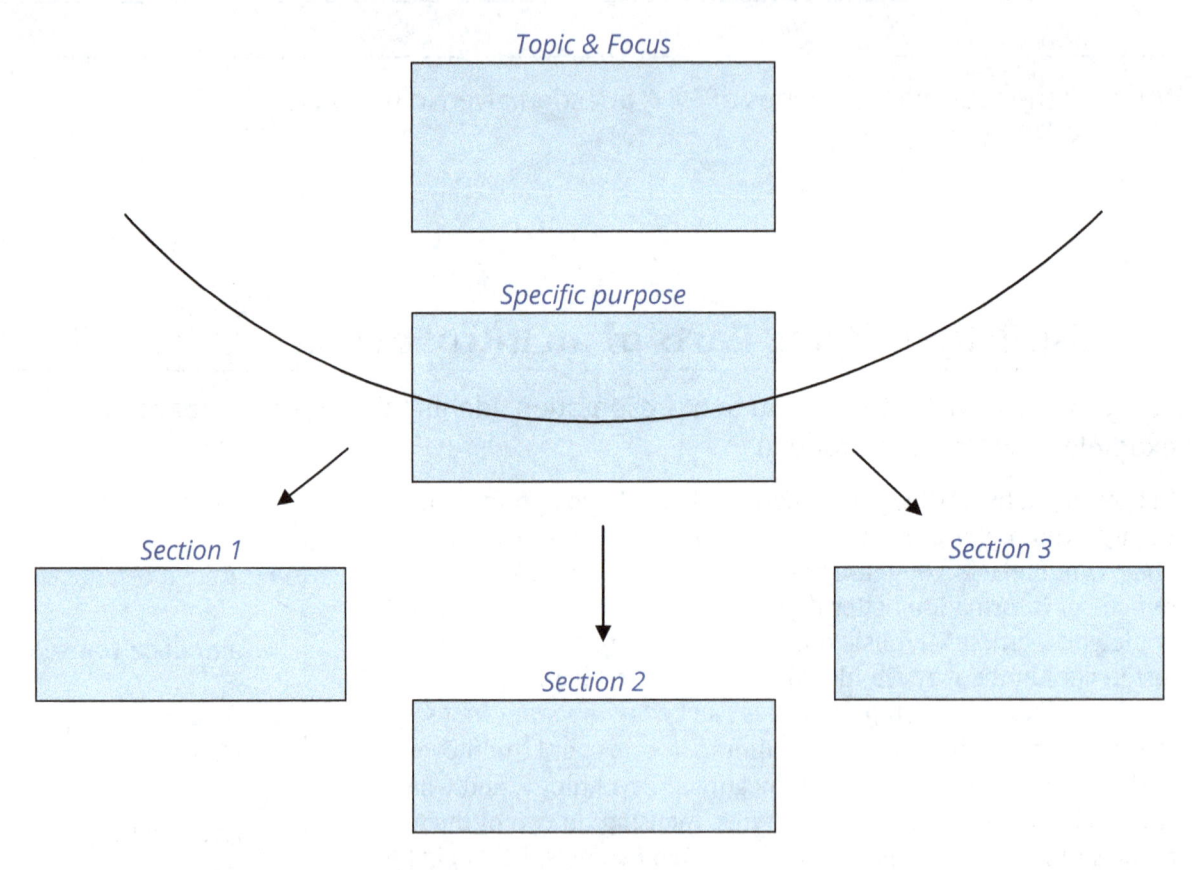

*Topic & Focus*

*Specific purpose*

*Section 1*

*Section 2*

*Section 3*

Note: If you found the mind map above helpful, you may want to use it to map out *your* own presentation. You can download a copy from the resources section of the website (see *Appendix 1*).

36

# Unit 2: **Structure**

## Exercise 4: **Q&A Question Types**

Study the following Q&A questions for a presentation on *Learning Styles*. Classify them according to the type of question they are. Choose from:

- Clarification
- Expansion
- Challenge
- Off-topic

| Question | Type |
| --- | --- |
| I didn't quite get what you said about the link between the Kolb learning cycle and learning styles. Can you explain? | |
| Are you sure that the Dunn and Dunn model is commonly used in teacher training in the USA? | |
| You talked about there being over 70 different models of learning styles. Can you give us some more examples? | |
| You talked about the VAK model, but I didn't quite catch what the letter K was for. Can tell us again? | |
| Why do you think students today are so bad at completing their homework? | |
| You've presented these styles as fact, but isn't it true that there is very little research to support them? | |
| Can you tell us the five dimensions of the Dunn and Dunn model again? | |
| You said that learning styles are important in teacher training courses. Where did you do your teacher training? | |
| You gave examples of how *visual* learners can improve their study. Could you give some more examples? | |
| Can you go over the history of learning styles one more time? | |

**EAP Foundation: Academic Presentations**

## Exercise 5: **Practice**

Practise giving your presentation, using the checklist in this unit to get feedback, either by assessing yourself or asking a peer to help you. If you have not yet finished preparing your presentation, return to this exercise later.

## Exercise 6: **Progress Check**

**First**, look back at *Exercise 4: Preparation* in Unit 1. Find any questions you highlighted because you could not answer them before. Can you answer any of these questions now? If so, record the answer.

**Then**, return to *Exercise 5: Planning your presentation* in Unit 1. Which stage should you be at now? Are you on track? Do you need to adjust the timing? Make a note of your progress (e.g. any stages which are now 'Started' or 'Complete') in the 'Progress' column.

# Unit 3: Language

## Learning Outcomes

By the end of this unit, you should:
- understand language to use in the introduction section;
- know how to state purpose, topic and focus;
- be able to use language to refer to visual aids;
- know some common transition phrases;
- know some other useful phrases (e.g. for giving examples, summarising);
- understand language for the conclusion section;
- understand language for different parts of the Q&A.

By completing the exercises, you will also:
- find and correct language errors in presentation phrases;
- begin to select phrases to use in your presentation;
- practise using language phrases for a real presentation topic;
- practise giving your presentation and get feedback on *language use*.

## Key Vocabulary

*Nouns*
- transition (*also a verb*)
- topic
- focus (*also a verb*)
- purpose
- objective (*also an adj*)
- aim (*also a verb*)

*Adjectives*
- formulaic

*Verbs*
- signpost (*also a noun*)

## Additional Vocabulary

*Academic Collocations*
- appropriate language (adj + n)
- crucial part (adj + n)
- technical problems (adj + n)
- vital part (adj + n)
- directly related (adv + past verb)

# EAP Foundation: Academic Presentations

## Overview

In this section you will find some language for presentations, also known as 'signpost' phrases, because they *signpost* (or *signal*) the direction of your talk. They are an example of formulaic language used in academic contexts, and many of these are similar to (or the same as) the lecture cues a lecturer uses.

You do not need to learn all of the phrases in this unit. Your basic aim is to be able to use at least one phrase for each function (e.g. expressing purpose and showing the structure in the introduction, using transitions between sections, referring to visual aids, concluding). How many more you learn after this is up to you. Presentations usually have many visual aids and several transitions between sections, so it would be useful to learn two or three different phrases for these functions. On the other hand, you will only state the purpose once in a presentation, so one phrase is enough for life!

## Language for introductions

The introduction is a crucial part of any presentation. As noted in Unit 2, there are several functions which you need to achieve, namely: arouse interest; greet the audience; introduce yourself; state the topic and focus; express the purpose; give the structure; give the timing; handle questions.

Phrases for all of these are given in the boxes on the next page, together with some explanation on the usage of some of them. As noted in the Introduction, the language phrases are shown in a way which minimises space and shows how the parts of the phrase can be combined. For example:

- My | presentation / talk | will | take / last | about 20 minutes.

These parts can be combined into four possible sentences, as follows:
- My <u>presentation</u> will <u>take</u> about 20 minutes.
- My <u>presentation</u> will <u>last</u> about 20 minutes.
- My <u>talk</u> will <u>take</u> about 20 minutes.
- My <u>talk</u> will <u>last</u> about 20 minutes.

# Unit 3: Language

**Arouse interest**
- Let me begin by asking you a question.
- Let me ask you a question.

▼

**Greet the audience**
- Good | morning / afternoon | ladies and gentlemen. / everyone.

▼

**Introduce yourself**
- I'm...
- My name is...

▼

Stating the topic and focus and expressing the purpose can be done separately or in one sentence. E.g.:
- *What I'm going to talk about today is the causes of global warming. My purpose is to explain the main causes.*
- *What I want to do today is explain the main causes of global warming.*

In both examples, the topic is *global warming*, the focus is *the main causes* and the purpose is *to explain*.

**State the topic and focus**
- What I'm going to talk about today is...
- What I want to look at today is... focusing on...

▼

**Express the purpose**
- My | purpose / objective / aim | today is to...
- What I want to do | this morning / this afternoon / today | is...
- I'm here today to...

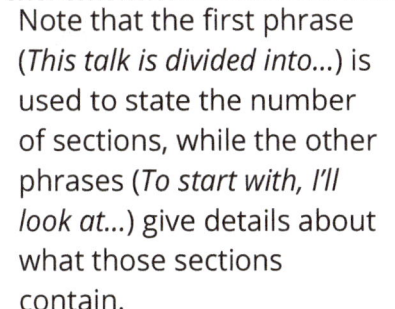

▼

Note that the first phrase (*This talk is divided into...*) is used to state the number of sections, while the other phrases (*To start with, I'll look at...*) give details about what those sections contain.

**Give the structure**
- This talk is divided into four main parts.
- To start with, | I'd like to look at...
- Then, | I'll look at...
- Thirdly... | I'll be talking about...
- Finally, | I'll be looking at...
- My | first / second / final | point will be about...

▼

**Give the timing**
- My | presentation / talk | will | take / last | about 20 minutes.

▼

**Handle questions**
- At the end of my talk, there will be a chance to ask questions.
- I'll be happy to answer any questions you have at the end of my presentation.

**EAP Foundation: Academic Presentations**

## Language for visual aids

It is important to be able to refer to your visual aids appropriately. On the right are some general phrases, which can be used for all types of visual aid, plus some specific ones for common types of visual aid (*slideware* and *handouts*).

> *For more on visual aids, see Unit 4: Visual Aids.* ▶▶

*General phrases*
- As you can see here...
- Here we can see...
- This | table / diagram / chart | shows...
- I'd like you to look at this.
- Let me show you...
- Let's look at...
- Let's take a look at...
- On the | right / left | you can see...
- At the | top / bottom | you can see...

*Phrases for slideware*
- If we look at this slide, we can see...
- If you look at the screen, you'll see...
- This slide shows...

*Phrases for handouts*
- If you look at the handout...
- If you turn to page 2 of the handout, you can see...

## Transition phrases

A vital part of any presentation is 'transitioning' or 'moving on' to a new section. Why is this so crucial? Mainly because of the difference between listening and reading. When you read, you can easily see where one section or paragraph ends and another begins. This

- Let's now / Let me now / I'd now like to / I now want to | move on to... / turn to... / go on to...
- Turning now to...
- This leads me to my next point, which is...

is not true when you listen. To help with this, good academic speakers, whether in presentations or lectures, give cues to signal the arrival of a new section and the end of the previous one. This helps the listener understand the structure and follow the main points.

# Unit 3: Language

Common transition phrases are shown in the box. Note that, as with transitions in lectures, words like 'OK' and 'Right' can be used in combination with these phrases, for example, 'OK, let's now go on to...' or 'Right, turning now to...'.

> *For more on how transition phrases are used by speakers in lectures, see EAP Foundation: Academic Listening.*

## Other phrases

There are some other phrases which are useful in a presentation. These include: giving examples; summarising a point or section; making a digression; handling technical problems; and resuming (after digression or technical problems).

Phrases for all of these are given to the right.

### Presentation Tip: Get on with it!
If you encounter technical problems, you can use the phrases in the box to 'buy time'. However, you cannot wait too long. If you can't recover from the problem after a short while, you will just have to give up and get on with the presentation. Likewise, if you choose to digress (probably best not to!), you should keep it short and get back to the main message as quickly as possible.

**Give examples**
- Let me give you an example...
- ... such as...
- ... for instance...
- A good example of this is...

**Summarise**
- What I'm trying to say is...
- Let me just try and sum that up before we move on...
- So far, I've presented...
- So far, I've told you about…

**Digress**
- I might just mention...
- Incidentally...

**Handle technical problems**
*Before the presentation starts*
- Sorry for the delay. We'll get started in just a moment.
- Sorry for this. Just bear with me while I get it fixed.

*During the presentation*
- Sorry about this. I'll have it fixed in just a second.

*After the problem is fixed*
- OK. Looks like everything's fine now.

**Resume (after digression or technical problem)**
- So as I was saying…
- Anyway, as I was saying…

**EAP Foundation: Academic Presentations**

# Language for concluding

The conclusion, like the introduction, has several functions which you need to achieve: sum up the main points of the presentation; conclude (by giving a 'take-away' message); close (by thanking the audience); invite questions.

Phrases for all of these are given below.

**Sum up**
- Summing up...
- To summarise...
- So, to sum up...
- To recap...
- Let me now sum up.

▼

**Conclude**
- Let me end by saying...
- I'd like to finish by emphasising...
- In | conclusion / closing | I'd like to say...
- Finally, may I say...

▼

**Close**
- Thank you for your | attention. / time.
- Thank you | for listening. / very much.

▼

**Invite questions**
- If you have any questions, I'll be happy to answer them now.
- If there are any questions, I'll do my best to answer them.

# Unit 3: Language

## Language for Q&A

During the Q&A you will answer questions from the audience. However, there are different types of response you can give (including saying that you do not know the answer!). You should generally check to ensure you understand the question, as well as check that your answer is satisfactory.

Useful phrases for the Q&A are given to the right.

**Clarifying with questioner**
- Do you mean...?

**Responding**
*If able to answer:*
- That's a great question.
- I'm glad you asked that question.
- I get asked that question by many people.

*If unable to answer:*
- I'm sorry, I'm not sure I can answer that question. Can I get back to you later?

*If off-topic:*
- That's an interesting question, but not directly related to what I've talked about. Maybe we can discuss that later.

**Checking answer is satisfactory**
- Does that answer your question?
- Is that the kind of information you were looking for?

**Continuing Q&A session**
- Are there any more questions?
- Does anyone have another question?

**Closing Q&A session**
- If there are no more questions I'll close by repeating my main message, which is...

# EAP Foundation: Academic Presentations

# Checklist

Below is a checklist for language. Use it to help you prepare, or ask a peer to use it to assess you when you practise.

| Section | Item | OK? | Comments |
|---|---|---|---|
| Introduction | The speaker uses appropriate language to:<br>• arouse interest;<br>• greet the audience;<br>• introduce him/herself;<br>• state the topic and focus;<br>• express the purpose;<br>• give the structure of the presentation;<br>• inform audience about timing;<br>• inform audience about handling questions. | | |
| Main body | The speaker:<br>• refers to visual aids using appropriate language;<br>• gives transitions between sections. | | |
| Conclusion | The speaker uses appropriate language to:<br>• sum up;<br>• conclude;<br>• thank the audience;<br>• invite questions. | | |
| Q&A | The speaker:<br>• clarifies/repeats questions (if necessary);<br>• responds to answers appropriately;<br>• checks answers are satisfactory;<br>• continues and closes the Q&A section appropriately. | | |

# Unit 3: Language

# Exercises

## Exercise 1: Comprehension

Answer the following questions about this unit. Either do this after reading the unit, or make notes first then use your notes to answer the questions.

1 What are 'signpost' phrases?
   _____
   _____

2 How many of the phrases in this unit do you need to learn?
   _____
   _____

3 Give two phrases for *stating the topic and focus*. Which *one* of these do you think you might use in your presentation?
   - 
   - 

4 Give two phrases for *stating the purpose*. Which *one* of these do you think you might use in your presentation?
   - 
   - 

5 What is the function of each of the following phrases?
   - Sorry about this. I'll have it fixed in just a second.   _____
   - Anyway, as I was saying…   _____
   - Let me give you an example…   _____
   - So far, I've presented…   _____

6 In which section would you normally use/hear these phrases?
   - That's a great question.   _____
   - Thank you very much.   _____
   - At the end of my talk, there will be a chance to ask questions   _____
   - Does that answer your question?   _____

47

**EAP Foundation: Academic Presentations**

## Exercise 2: **Language for Introductions**

**a)** Below are phrases for use in an *Introduction*. However, each sentence has an *error*, either a wrong word, a missing word, or wrong word form. Find and correct the error. An example has been done for you.

               *is*
My name <u>are</u>...

What I want to talk today is...

The purpose of my presentation is give an overview of...

Let me begin by ask you a question.

This talk divides into three main parts.

My presentation takes about 15 minutes.

I'll be happy to answer some questions you have at the end of my presentation.

**b)** The following phrases can all be used in the *Introduction* to a presentation. Complete the phrases by adding the missing words. There may be more than one possibility for each gap; choose *any* word which is appropriate.

Good _____, everyone.

My _____ today is to...

To _____ with, I'd like to look at...

My fourth _____ will be about...

Finally, I'll be _____ at...

**c)** Identify which language function each phrase in **a)** and **b)** above is for (e.g. *state the topic*).

# Unit 3: Language

## Exercise 3: **Language for Main Body**

Read the following extracts (A-C) from a presentation. Each extract contains the end of one section and the beginning of another. For each extract:
- find the break and mark it with //;
- find and underline all of the signpost language phrases;
- identify the function of each phrase you have underlined;
- decide which order the extracts go in (they are **not** in the correct order).

A   This particular theory of learning styles is especially common in training courses in the USA. Having looked at the two main styles, I'd like to move on to my final area, which is considering how these styles can be used to improve your own learning. As we have seen, each of us prefers to learn in a different way, and if we can be more aware of *how* we prefer to learn…

B   …which led to interest in different styles. Some studies suggest there are over 70 such styles in total. Right, let's now move on now to the second area, which is a detailed look at the two main models of learning styles, beginning with the VAK model. This model is probably the most well-known…

C   … please feel free to ask me at the end. OK, so let me begin by talking a little about the history of learning styles. Learning styles first became prominent in the field of education in the mid-1970s…

## Exercise 4: **Language for Transitions and Visuals**

Match the following sentence halves to create phrases for *transitions* and *referring to visuals*. Then, label them (T) if they are *transition phrases*, or (V) if they are for *visuals*. An example has been done for you.

| | | | | |
|---|---|---|---|---|
| a | This leads me to | i | turn to… | |
| b | As you | ii | show you… | |
| c | Here | iii | look at this. | (V) |
| d | I'd now like to move | iv | my next point… | |
| e | This table | v | to go on to… | |
| f | Let me | vi | shows… | |
| g | Let's now | vii | on to… | |
| h | I now want | viii | can see here… | |
| i | I'd like you to | ix | we can see… | |

49

# EAP Foundation: Academic Presentations

## Exercise 5: **Language for Conclusions**

The following phrases can all be used in the *Conclusion* of a presentation.

**First**, complete the phrases by adding the missing words. There may be more than one possibility for each gap; choose *any* word which is appropriate.

So, to _____...

Let me _____ by saying...

Thank you for your _____.

If you have any _____ I'll be happy to answer them now.

**Then**, match each phrase to one of the functions of a Conclusion (e.g. *invite questions*).

## Exercise 6: **Personalising the Language**

Look back at the language phrases in this unit. Highlight the ones you think you might use in your presentation. Write some of the more difficult ones in the table below (writing them out will help you remember). Also make a note of the function (e.g. *state the purpose*).

| Phrases I like | Function |
| --- | --- |
|  |  |
|  |  |
|  |  |
|  |  |
|  |  |
|  |  |

# Unit 3: Language

## Exercise 7: Practice

Practise giving your presentation, using the checklist in this unit to get feedback. Practice each section separately, as many times as you need to, paying attention to the language phrases. Try to use the ones you noted in Exercise 6 above, if you have completed that exercise. Practise until you can use these phrases fluently. If you do not have a presentation to work on, you can use the outline in *Appendix 6: Presentation Outline*.

> What I want to talk about today is…

## Exercise 8: Progress check

**First**, look back at *Exercise 4: Preparation* in Unit 1. Find any questions you highlighted because you could not answer them before. Can you answer any of these questions now? If so, record the answer.

**Then**, return to *Exercise 5: Planning your presentation* in Unit 1. Which stage should you be at now? Are you on track? Do you need to adjust the timing? Make a note of your progress (e.g. any stages which are now 'Started' or 'Complete') in the 'Progress' column.

**EAP Foundation: Academic Presentations**

# Unit 4: **Visual Aids**

## Learning Outcomes

By the end of this unit, you should:
- be aware of different types of visual aid (slideware, handout, etc.);
- know some advantages and disadvantages of each type;
- understand different ways to present information in visual aids (table, bar chart, pie chart, etc.);
- understand when each way is appropriate (e.g. table for contrasting);
- know some best practices for making visual aids *visual*;
- know some best practices for ensuring visual aids *aid*;
- be familiar with some language to use when presenting visual information.

By completing the exercises, you will also:
- assess risk involved with each type of visual aid;
- create PowerPoint slides, using textual information;
- create different types of visual, using numerical data;
- peer assess other students' visuals;
- correct problems in PowerPoint slides;
- practise giving your presentation and get feedback on *visual aids*.

## Vocabulary

Key vocabulary for this unit:
**Nouns**
- visual (*also an adj*)
- aid (*also a verb*)
- slideware
- handout
- flipchart
- bar chart
- pie chart
- diagram

## Additional Vocabulary

*Academic Collocations*
- appropriate language (adj + n)
- common approach (adj + n)
- technical problems (adj + n)
- useful information (adj + n)
- describe a process (v + n)
- encounter problems (v + n)

**EAP Foundation: Academic Presentations**

## Overview

A visual aid is anything which your audience can see and which helps them to follow your spoken presentation. In addition to aiding understanding, visual aids can help to keep the audience's attention and interest by adding variety to the presentation style; however interesting the speaker, it is difficult to remain interested for long if that speaker does nothing but talk to the audience.

## Types of visual aid

There are several different types of visual aid you can use in an academic presentation. Each has its advantages and disadvantages. Some of these visual aids can be used in combination, the most common being slideware (PowerPoint) with video or handouts, though other combinations are possible, such as poster with real object or slideware with whiteboard.

**1. Slideware**
Slideware means software for showing slides. This is the most common type of visual aid. Examples are PowerPoint (also called PPT) and Keynote. This type of visual aid needs a computer and projector, and the chance of encountering problems is high, for instance broken laptop, missing PPT file, bad connection between laptop and computer.

> *Some of these problems (and the ones given below) are considered in Unit 1, Exercise 2: Solving Common Problems.*

**2. Whiteboard or blackboard**
A whiteboard (or blackboard) can be a useful visual aid. Writing on a whiteboard (or blackboard) is more engaging than PowerPoint because it is 'live', meaning your words are written at the time rather than in advance. One problem with this type of visual is that your back will be facing the audience when you are writing. A whiteboard (or blackboard) is especially useful when brainstorming ideas from the audience or when drawing a diagram. You should consider beforehand whether you will erase the words when finished or leave them on the board. Both can be distracting. If you plan to use a whiteboard or blackboard you should, of course, check the room first to make sure one is installed. The chance of

encountering problems with a whiteboard or blackboard is fairly low, though still exists, for example lack of whiteboard pens (or chalk) for writing, pens that have no ink, missing eraser, or an old whiteboard which smears when you try to erase.

## 3. Handouts

Handouts can be a useful visual aid if you have lots of information to give the audience. Your PowerPoint may summarise the main points while the handout gives more detail. Deciding when to give out the handout is important, because once the audience has the handout, they may want to read it instead of listening, especially when you first give it out. A common approach to handouts, especially for lectures (rather than presentations) is for the speaker to give out copies of their PowerPoint slides. Although this gives the audience something to take notes on, it makes the PowerPoint rather pointless, as the audience has all of the information from the outset. For this reason, it is probably not a good approach for presentations. The problems you are most likely to encounter if using handouts are with a copier when preparing copies, or not preparing enough handouts.

> **Presentation Tip: Timing**
> The following is some advice for when to give out a handout.
> - If listeners will need to refer to the handout, you should give it out either at the beginning, or in the middle when you first need it.
> - If listeners will not need to refer to the handout, giving it out at the end is best.
> - If possible, give out your handout in sections rather than all at once, though beware of giving out too many, which may become tiresome for the audience.

## 4. Flipchart

A flipchart is a large pad of paper on a stand. You will usually write information during your talk, though it is possible to prepare this beforehand. For best effect, you should plan or at least have some idea what you will write. You should keep to one main idea per sheet. Advantages of using a flipchart are, first, it is easy to go back and forth, and second, it does not need power, meaning you are unlikely to encounter any problems. It is only really suitable for a small audience.

## 5. Video

Video can be very powerful, though in a presentation you will usually need to keep it short. It needs equipment, usually a computer and projector, though TV and DVD player are also possible. Video is usually used in combination with another visual aid, and it is possible to embed video in a PowerPoint presentation.

> **Presentation Tip: Reducing risk**
> Some visual aids have a risk of problems. Try to reduce risk, e.g.:
> - if you plan to use slideware, use your own laptop;
> - if you plan to use handouts, copy well in advance;
> - if you plan to use online video, e.g. from YouTube, download it first.

# EAP Foundation: Academic Presentations

**6. Real objects**
Showing the audience real, physical objects (also known as *realia*) can be helpful. It needs to be large enough for the audience to see. You might want to pass it around, which will take up time, so plan for this. You will probably want to keep it concealed before you use it.

**7. Prezi**
Prezi is similar to *shareware*. It requires you to plot themes and add visual content, allowing you to demonstrate connections that would not be as clear if you were using PowerPoint. Some people, however, find Prezi too 'busy' and therefore distracting.

**8. Poster**
A poster can be a good visual aid if the audience is small, for example a dozen people. If the audience is large, the poster may not be visible for those at the back. It can be a useful visual aid for group work in class, as it can be completed and displayed during a lesson more easily than a PowerPoint presentation. As all the information will be on one (usually large) sheet of paper, some thought needs to be given to the poster design. This visual aid is very low-tech, which means the chance of encountering problems is extremely low.

## What to present in visual aids

There are many ways to present the information via a visual aid. These include:
- graph;
- table;
- bar chart;
- pie chart;
- diagram;
- photograph;
- text.

Your choice of which to use will usually depend on the type of data or information you are presenting. A graph can be useful for showing changes over time. If you are contrasting two items, a table is useful, as the audience will be able to see the information side by side. A bar chart is also used for comparing two or more items, though this type of graph is for numbers rather than information. A pie chart is generally used to show percentage or proportional data, adding up to 100%. A diagram is useful for describing a process or showing how something works, while a photograph is ideal for showing real examples. Finally, text is what will make up most of your visual aid content – but try to keep it brief (see *Guidelines for visuals* on the next page for more information on this).

# Unit 4: Visual Aids

## Guidelines for visuals

Remember that visual aids must be *visual*, i.e. 'able to be seen'. You should make sure the visuals can be seen by everyone in the audience, including those at the back of the room. When designing your visual aid (especially PowerPoint), you should think carefully about colour and size; light background and dark lettering is usually best. A minimum font size of 24 is recommended. Visual aids summarise information and make it more immediately understandable, so if it is possible to use a graph or diagram or other visual in place of text, you should do so.

> **In short**
> Make your visual aids **visual**:
> - check that the audience at the back can see;
> - be careful with colour and size (white background/dark lettering, font size 24 or more);
> - use graphs or diagrams in place of words wherever possible.

Remember also that your visual aid must *aid* or 'help' your presentation. Your PowerPoint slides should back up your verbal message, for example by having one which shows the structure (in the Introduction), another with a summary (in the Conclusion), and others in between which give the key points that you want to make. The part about *key points* is important; your visual aid should *aid* the presentation, not take its place. You will add details while you speak, and if you have too much detail in the visual aid your audience may spend too much time reading it rather than listening to you (it is difficult to both read and listen at the same time). Some writers refer to the six-by-six rule, meaning a maximum of six lines of text, with a maximum of six words per line. This is rather restrictive and can be difficult to stick to, meaning you will break the rule a lot of the time; nonetheless, it is a useful general guideline. Another point to consider here is to make sure you only include visuals which add to your overall message (a cute picture might get a laugh, but if it is not relevant, you should not include it). Finally, you should make sure that all of the information contained in the visual is referred to in your talk; otherwise, the extra information may prove distracting.

> **In short**
> Make sure your visual aids **aid** your presentation:
> - include slides for structure and summary;
> - include only key points;
> - consider the six-by-six rule;
> - make sure all images give useful information;
> - refer to all information in the visual during the talk.

Two other points to consider when creating visual aids are consistency and appropriateness. If you are using PowerPoint, you should make sure your slides are consistent by using a 'parallel' structure. For example, if your first bullet point on a slide is a noun, the other bullet points should be too. Consistency is also important if you are working as part of a group. Make sure all group members use the same format for their PowerPoint or other visuals. Appropriateness means choosing the right way to display the information, such as using a table to compare. See *What to present in visual aids* above for more information on this.

## Referring to visuals

It is important, when using visual aids, to refer to them using appropriate language. Some examples are given below. More can be found in *Unit 3: Language*.

- As you can see here…
- Here we can see…
- If we look at this slide…
- This slide shows…

## Checklist

Below is a checklist for visual aids. Use it to help you prepare, or ask a peer to use it to assess you when you practise.

| Item | OK? | Comments |
| --- | --- | --- |
| The choice of visual aid(s) is/are appropriate. | | |
| Information is presented in a suitable way (e.g. table for contrasting, chart or graph for data). | | |
| Information and images are big enough to be seen from the back. | | |
| Data have been appropriately selected for charts/tables (not too much). | | |
| There is the right amount of text (6-by-6 rule). | | |
| Colour is OK (e.g. light background, dark letters). | | |
| Visual aids cover all main points. | | |
| There is a visual which shows the structure. | | |
| There is a visual which summarises the main points. | | |
| All images give useful information. | | |
| All information in the visual aid is also in the talk. | | |
| There are not too many slides/images/handouts. | | |
| There were no technical problems. | | |

# Unit 4: Visual Aids

# Exercises

## Exercise 1: Comprehension

Answer the following questions about this unit. Either do this after reading the unit, or make notes first then use the notes to answer the questions.

1 The following chart summarises the information for each type of visual aid. Use the information in the unit to complete the gaps.

**8. Poster**
- Especially useful for xv) _____ audience.
- Good for xvi) _____.
- Think about xvii) _____ before making it.

**1. i)** _____
- Most common.
- E.g. ii) _____ and Keynote.
- Needs computer and projector.

**2. Whiteboard/blackboard**
- More engaging than PPT.
- Especially useful for iii) _____.
- iv) _____ when finished, but check.

**7. Prezi**
- Similar to xiii) _____.
- Shows xiv) _____.
- May be too 'busy' for some people.

**Types of visual aid**

**3. Handouts**
- Useful if lots of v) _____.
- Think carefully about vi) _____.

**6. xi)** _____ **object**
- Needs to be xii) _____ enough.

**5. Video**
- Very x) _____.
- Needs equipment (computer and projector or TV and DVD player).

**4. Flipchart**
- Write during talk, or vii) _____.
- Easy to viii) _____.
- Does not need ix) _____.

# EAP Foundation: Academic Presentations

2 Match the following types of information with the best way to present each one. Choose from:
- graph
- table
- bar chart
- pie chart
- diagram
- photograph
- text

| Type of information | Best way to present it |
| --- | --- |
| Information on the main factors of the US economy compared to those of the Indian economy. | |
| A demonstration of how to conduct a simple laboratory experiment. | |
| Information on the factors which contribute to GDP. | |
| Month-by-month data on the US dollar-UK pound exchange rate from 2015 to 2017. | |
| An example of the damage suffered by buildings in Dresden during aerial bombings in WWII. | |
| The percentage of students who prefer different types of hobby (totalling 100%). | |
| A comparison of total revenue from imports (in US$) for China and Japan, in 2000, 2005, 2010 and 2015. | |

3 Why is the colour of background and lettering of a visual aid important?
_____
_____

4 Why might the size of text in a visual be an issue?
_____
_____

5 What is the recommended size of text for PPT?
_____
_____

# Unit 4: **Visual Aids**

**6** Why should you include a visual (e.g. PPT slide) showing the structure, and another giving a summary?

_____
_____

**7** Why might having too much text in your visual be a problem?

_____
_____

**8** What is the name of the 'rule' related to the amount of text in the visual?

_____
_____

**9** What is wrong with using a cute (but unrelated) picture in your presentation?

_____
_____

**10** What does *consistency* mean in relation to visual aids?

_____
_____

## Exercise 2: **Assessing Risk**

Put each of the visual aids on the diagram below to show how likely each one is to encounter problems. Choose from:

- slideware
- flipchart
- handouts
- whiteboard
- video
- real object
- prezi
- poster

Very low chance — Low chance — Moderate chance — High chance — Very high chance

# EAP Foundation: Academic Presentations

## Exercise 3: **Creating PowerPoint slides**

Read this information on *GDP* and *GNP*. Use it to create two PowerPoint slides (at the end of the page). To complete this task, you should:
- follow the *6-by-6 rule* as far as possible (but OK to break it!);
- use a *parallel structure* for consistency (e.g. all noun phrases);
- add bullet points, as appropriate;
- select information (do not try to include everything).

The size of a nation's overall economy is typically measured by its *gross domestic product (GDP)*, which is the value of all final goods and services produced within a country in a given year. The measurement of GDP involves counting up the production of millions of different goods and services—smart phones, cars, music downloads, computers, steel, bananas, college educations, and all other new goods and services produced in the current year—and summing them into a total value. Each of the market transactions that enter into GDP must involve both a buyer and a seller. The GDP of an economy can therefore be measured either by the total value of what is purchased in the economy, or by the total value of what is produced.

Besides GDP, there are two different but closely related ways of measuring the size of the economy. One of the closest measurements to GDP is the *gross national product (GNP)*. GDP includes only what is produced within a country's borders. GNP adds what is produced by domestic businesses and labour abroad, and subtracts any payments sent home to other countries by foreign labour and businesses located in the country. For the United States, the gap between GDP and GNP is relatively small; in recent years, only about 0.2%. For small nations, which may have a significant proportion of their population working abroad and sending money back home, the difference can be substantial.

*Extracts taken from Principles of Economics, ©2017 Rice University. Download for free at https://openstax.org/details/books/principles-economics*

**GDP**

**GNP**

# Unit 4: **Visual Aids**

## Exercise 4: **Creating visuals**

Use one of the data sets in *Appendix 4: Data for visual aids* to create *at least two* different visuals. You might like to use the related presentation topic in *Appendix 3: Presentation topics* to help you focus on the task.

To complete this exercise, you should follow these steps.
1. Decide on your focus for the task.
2. Select relevant data.
3. Decide *how* you will present the information (table etc.).
4. Create a rough plan of your visuals. A4 paper would be best for this planning stage. You should think about headings for your visuals, and choose colouring. Make sure you are happy with your visuals before moving to the next stage.
5. Prepare your visuals for presentation to other students. This will mean making sure they are *visual* e.g. by preparing a PowerPoint presentation (if you have access to a computer and projector), or copying the visual to a larger piece of paper (at least A3 size).
6. Present the information in the visual aids to other students. Use the following checklist to assess other students' visuals. This is adapted from the earlier version, with new items – which relate specifically to this exercise – in *italics*.

| Item | Rating | Comments |
|---|---|---|
| *At least two different visuals are used.* | 1 2 3 4 5 | |
| Information is presented in a suitable way (e.g. table for contrasting, chart or graph for data). | 1 2 3 4 5 | |
| Information and images are big enough to be seen from the back. | 1 2 3 4 5 | |
| Data have been appropriately selected for charts/tables (not too much). | 1 2 3 4 5 | |
| There is the right amount of text (6-by-6 rule). | 1 2 3 4 5 | |
| Colour is OK (e.g. light background, dark letters). | 1 2 3 4 5 | |
| All information in the visual aid is also in the talk. | 1 2 3 4 5 | |
| *Headings for visuals are concise and appropriate.* | 1 2 3 4 5 | |
| **TOTAL** | ___ / 40 | |

# EAP Foundation: Academic Presentations

## Exercise 5: **Improving visual aids**

Access the online resources (see *Appendix 1*). You will find some PowerPoint examples. Look through each one and find and correct problems. [Full instructions are given in the PowerPoint.]

## Exercise 6: **Practice**

Practise giving your presentation, using the checklist in this unit to get feedback, either by assessing yourself or asking a peer to help you. If you have not yet finished preparing your presentation, return to this exercise later.

## Exercise 7: **Progress Check**

**First**, look back at *Exercise 4: Preparation* in Unit 1. Find any questions you highlighted because you could not answer them before. Can you answer any of these questions now? If so, record the answer.

**Then**, return to *Exercise 5: Planning your presentation* in Unit 1. Which stage should you be at now? Are you on track? Do you need to adjust the timing? Make a note of your progress (e.g. any stages which are now 'Started' or 'Complete') in the 'Progress' column.

# Part III:
## Performance

# Unit 5: Body Language

## Learning Outcomes

By the end of this unit, you should:
- understand element of good body language (position, posture, movement, eye contact);
- know how to position yourself when delivering a presentation;
- understand why good posture is important;
- understand why movement is important;
- be aware of different types of movement to consider (body, face/head, hands);
- understand why eye contact is important.

By completing the exercises, you will also:
- practise using hand movement to add meaning;
- check your eye contact when presenting;
- practise giving your presentation and get feedback on *body language*.

## Vocabulary

Key vocabulary for this unit:

*Nouns*
- posture
- position (*also a verb*)
- movement
- eye contact
- gesture (*also a verb*)
- expression

## Additional Vocabulary

*Academic Collocations*
- facial expressions (adj + n)
- give a presentation (v + n)

# EAP Foundation: Academic Presentations

## Overview

The main message in your presentation is contained in the words you use, and will be very clear to you. The message you give with your body, however, may be less clear, and might be very different from the one you intend. This is only natural: you can hear everything you say, but you cannot see yourself saying it. It is often said that body language is *more* important than the verbal message. While this may be true if you are giving a presentation in the business world and are trying to sell a product or service, for an academic presentation the content is always more important. However boring the presentation, the audience still has to listen and try to follow what you are telling them. The main reason to focus on body language during an academic presentation is that clear, confident body language makes the presentation more interesting, which makes the audience listen more closely, which means they are more likely to understand and remember the main points.

Body language, both good and bad, involves many different elements. The most important ones are position, posture, movement and eye contact. Each is considered in more detail below.

> **Presentation Tip: Look vs feel**
> It is useful to remember that looking confident and feeling confident are not the same. Almost everyone gets nervous when they have to speak in public, but not everyone shows it. Use good body language to help you appear confident, even if you are not!

## Position

The most important thing to remember about delivering a presentation is: face the audience! The collocation 'give a presentation' is important. Think of 'give a present' or 'give a gift'. You would not give someone a present with your back to them, and yet many speakers give a presentation this way, because they spend too much time talking to the screen or whiteboard or their notes. This is sometimes the result of nerves, and sometimes the result of not being familiar enough with the material (the solution to both of these problems is:

> **In short**
> Position:
> - face the audience;
> - if you need to look at the screen or whiteboard, stop talking.

68

# Unit 5: **Body Language**

*rehearse*). If you do need to turn away while presenting, for example to look at the screen and find some information, then stop talking, look at the screen first, and face the audience again when you continue speaking.

## Posture

Your posture (also called stance) relates to how you stand. In a presentation, you should try to stand up straight. This not only helps you look more confident but will also allow you to control your breathing and voice production. In other words, you will look better, feel better and sound better. It is important to think about where your hands will be and what you will do with them. You may sometimes use them for gesturing (see next), though most of the time your hands will either be in front of your body or behind your back; choose which is most natural for you.

> **In short**
> Posture:
> - stand up straight;
> - think about your hands – in front or behind.

## Movement

Audiences respond best to presenters who are energetic, and in order to convey that energy to the audience you need to move. There are three types of movement to consider during a presentation. The first is movement of your *body*. This type of movement should not be exaggerated; too much can be distracting. You should make sure your body movement has a purpose. For example, you might approach the projector screen to point something out, or you might move closer to the audience in order to make them feel more included.

> **In short**
> You can display energy by:
> - moving your body (towards the screen, approach the audience);
> - moving your face (smile) and head (nod);
> - moving your hands (stress, count, express something physical);
> - be aware of your nervous gestures and control them.

The second type of movement is movement of your *face* or *head*. These are very expressive parts of your body, and you should take care to ensure that your facial expressions and head movements are positive. You will want to smile – especially at the beginning – and you may nod in response to a comment from an audience member.

The final type of movement to consider is movement of your *hands*. You may use your hands in a general way, for example to stress important points, or you may use them to express something specific, for example to count, to express something big (hands held wide apart) or something small (hands held close together). This latter type of hand movement is also called 'gestural vocabulary', and is generally the same whatever language you are speaking. Nervous speakers have nervous hands, which slip into pockets, touch

# EAP Foundation: Academic Presentations

hair or play with glasses. Being aware of your nervous gestures (ask a peer to watch out) will help you to control them better during the presentation.

If you are speaking in a large room, with a podium, there may be much less scope for movement. This tends to be the case for speeches rather than presentations, though some conference presentations may be delivered in this way. If possible, try to move away from the podium so that you will have more room to move. If you must stand behind the podium, at least try to hold the sides of the podium so that the audience can see your hands.

## Eye contact

Eye contact is important because it creates a relationship between the speaker and the audience. It encourages the audience to listen, and it helps the speaker to relax. It can also help you to understand whether the audience is following, for example if they nod, which may increase your confidence. Making good eye contact can be difficult as you may not be used to addressing so many people at the same time. A good strategy is to focus on one person at a time and hold their eyes for as long as it takes to complete a natural phrase. Make sure you include members from each side of the room (many speakers tend to focus mostly on one side), and try to make eye contact with each person at least once during the presentation.

> **In short**
> Eye contact:
> - focus on one person at a time;
> - make sure you look at both sides of the room;
> - try to make eye contact with everyone at least once.

Unit 5: **Body Language**

# Checklist

Below is a checklist for body language. Ask a peer to use it to assess you when you practise. (This is a difficult area to self-assess, though you could do this if you are able to video yourself, e.g. on a mobile phone.)

| Area | Item | OK? | Comments |
| --- | --- | --- | --- |
| **Posture** | Posture is confident (standing up straight). | | |
| | Hands are held in a comfortable position. | | |
| **Position** | Position is good (facing the audience, not talking to the screen or notes). | | |
| **Movement** | Body movement is natural (not too much or too little). | | |
| | Head and facial movement is positive (nodding, smiling). | | |
| | Hand movement is natural, e.g. to emphasise points, to count, to demonstrate. | | |
| | Nervous gestures (touching hair/glasses) are avoided. | | |
| **Eye contact** | Eye contact is maintained throughout the presentation. | | |
| | The speaker looks at the whole audience (not just one or two people). | | |
| | The speaker avoids talking to the screen/notes. | | |

**EAP Foundation: Academic Presentations**

# Exercises

## Exercise 1: Comprehension

Answer the following questions about this unit. Either do this after reading the unit, or make notes first then use your notes to answer the questions.

1 Why might your body's message be less clear to you than your verbal message?

2 Correct this sentence: *Good speakers are confident.*

3 How should you *position* yourself when giving a presentation?

4 What should you do if you need to look at the screen?

5 What are the benefits of good *posture*?

6 Why is *movement* important during a presentation?

7 What types of *movement* should you be aware of during a presentation?
   - 
   - 
   - 

8 What is the problem with *too much* movement?

# Unit 5: **Body Language**

**9** What is 'gestural vocabulary'? Give examples.

_____

_____

_____

**10** Why is *eye contact* important?

_____

_____

\* \* \* \* \*

Note: The best way to improve areas of *performance* (i.e. *body language* – Unit 5 – and *delivery* – Unit 6) is by *performing* and getting feedback. Most exercises in this unit and the next one therefore assume you have a presentation you are able to practise. If you do not yet have a complete presentation, it is sufficient to practise only *part* of it, for example the Introduction. If you do not have a presentation ready to practise, you can use the outline given in *Appendix 6: Presentation outline*.

\* \* \* \* \*

## Exercise 2: **Hand Movement**

Look at the following summary of *movement* from the unit above. **First**, find words or phrases you could use hand gestures to emphasise or clarify.

> There are three types of movement to consider during a presentation. The first is movement of your body. Too much body movement can be distracting, so make sure not to move around too much. The second type of movement is movement of your face or head. These are very expressive parts of your body, and you should take care to ensure that your facial expressions and head movements are positive. The third and final type of movement to consider is movement of your hands. This type of movement can have a big effect on whether you look confident or not.

**Then**, read out this section, using your hands as appropriate. Ask a peer to give feedback, focusing on these questions.
- Were hand gestures appropriate?
- Were there enough/too many/too few gestures?
- Were there any nervous gestures? If so, what?

# EAP Foundation: Academic Presentations

## Exercise 3: **Eye Contact**

Use the summary of *movement* from Exercise 2 again. **First**, make a note of the main points (do not just read the text or you will not have good eye contact). **Then**, spend some time to remember them (again, to avoid reading and increase eye contact). **Finally**, present the information to a group of classmates (at least three). Ask a peer to give feedback, focusing on these questions.

- Does the speaker look at all members of the audience?
- Does the speaker look at all members equally, or does (s)he focus mainly on one person?
- Does the speaker look at the audience when speaking? If not at the audience, where does (s)he look (e.g. notes or in the air)?

## Exercise 4: **Practice**

Practise giving your presentation, using the checklist in this unit to get feedback, either by assessing yourself or asking a peer to help you. It is enough to practise just one section, for example the Introduction, in order to get feedback. If you do not have a presentation to work on, you can use the outline presentation in *Appendix 6: Presentation Outline*.

## Exercise 5: **Progress Check**

**First**, look back at *Exercise 4: Preparation* in Unit 1. Find any questions you highlighted because you could not answer them before. Can you answer any of these questions now? If so, record the answer.

**Then**, return to *Exercise 5: Planning your presentation* in Unit 1. Which stage should you be at now? Are you on track? Do you need to adjust the timing? Make a note of your progress (e.g. any stages which are now 'Started' or 'Complete') in the 'Progress' column.

# Unit 6: Delivery

## Learning Outcomes

By the end of this unit, you should:
- understand factors which affect delivery (pace, pronunciation, volume and emphasis);
- know the correct pace for a presentation;
- understand how to improve your pronunciation for presentations;
- understand why volume is important;
- know about possible sources of noise which could disrupt your presentation;
- understand how to add emphasis to words;
- know the difference between content and function words;
- understand which type of word should be emphasised.

By completing the exercises, you will also:
- identify words which should be stressed;
- practise stressing important words;
- identify key words in your talk and focus on their pronunciation;
- practise giving your presentation and get feedback on *delivery*.

## Key Vocabulary

**Nouns**
- pace (*also a verb*)
- pronunciation
- volume
- emphasis
- stress (*also a verb*)
- content
- function (*also a verb*)

**Verbs**
- emphasise

**Adjectives**
- rehearsed
- spontaneous

## Additional Vocabulary

*ACL (Academic Collocation List) words*
- key factors (adj + n)
- place emphasis (on) (v + n)

# EAP Foundation: Academic Presentations

## Overview

The final area to consider is delivery. One of the key factors in the delivery of an effective presentation is something which you do not need to learn, you simply need to do, and that is: *practise*. The more you practise, the more familiar you will become with the content of your presentation, and the more fluent and natural your delivery is likely to be. There are, however, certain factors which will improve the delivery of your presentation and which you should focus on when practising. They are pace, pronunciation, volume and emphasis.

## Pace

If you are nervous, you will probably find yourself speaking more quickly than usual. This is the wrong thing to do. Listening is a difficult skill, and your audience needs time to both hear and understand your main points. You should therefore aim to speak a little more slowly than usual. A general rule is: the larger the audience, the more slowly you need to speak. Speaking more slowly will also help to calm your nerves. This does not mean your presentation should be slow and steady throughout, as you will vary the pace by emphasising key words (see *Emphasis* below). Another reason to speak more slowly is that it will help you to focus on pronunciation (see next section), which is important if you are not confident about this area.

> **In short**
> To control the **pace**, you should:
> - speak a little more slowly than normal;
> - the larger the audience, the more slowly you should speak;
> - also speak more slowly if you are worried about your pronunciation.

## Pronunciation

Pronunciation in presentations is essentially the same as in general speech. The main difference comes from the fact that a presentation is *rehearsed*, in contrast to ordinary speech which is *spontaneous*. This means that you will know in advance what you will talk about, and in particular, what the key words will be. These are the ones you need to say correctly, because if the audience does not understand the key words, they will struggle to understand your main ideas. If possible, make a list of the key words before you give your presentation, check their pronunciation (in a dictionary, with a teacher), and make sure you can say them correctly during your talk. Focus not just on the vowel and consonant sounds, but also the position of the stress (called 'word stress'), which can often change when word form changes, e.g.:

> **In short**
> To improve **pronunciation**:
> - identify key words;
> - make sure you know how to say them correctly.

o O          o o o O o
*pronounce*        *pronunciation*

# Unit 6: Delivery

## Volume

You need to make sure that everyone in the room can hear you *comfortably*. This word is important: if you are too quiet and audience members need to strain to hear, it is not comfortable, any more than if you are shouting at the audience. If you are unsure of the right volume, it is definitely better to be too loud than too quiet: if you are too loud, it may be annoying, but at least the audience can still hear your message. If the room is large it can be useful to ask audience members at the back whether they can hear you; not only will this ensure your volume is loud enough, but it will help to create a connection with the audience before your presentation begins. It can be helpful to consider seating arrangements before your presentation to ensure you do not have to talk any louder than necessary. People will often fill up seats at the back, even though there is plenty of space at the front. If there are more seats than people, think about blocking out the back seats so audience members have to sit towards the front; alternatively, ask them to move forward.

> **In short**
> For the ideal **volume**:
> - speak a little louder than you think is necessary;
> - project your voice to the back of the room;
> - check that people at the back can hear;
> - if people are sitting too far back, consider asking them to move forward.

> **Presentation Tip: Keep the noise down!**
> There are many sources of noise which can disturb a presentation. Some may come from outside (through open windows or door), some from inside (audience members talking), some from yourself (nervous tapping of your pen). Close the door and window, ask audience members to keep quiet, and watch out for your nervous noises!

⏪ *See* Venue *in* Unit 1: Preparation and Planning *for questions about the venue, including rearranging the furniture before your talk.*

## Emphasis

When you are writing, you can emphasise (or 'stress') your main points by using **bold** type or *italics*. When you are speaking you also need to place emphasis on the important words or ideas. In speech, this is done by:
- saying the word more slowly;
- saying the word more loudly;
- pausing briefly before and after the word.

# EAP Foundation: Academic Presentations

This kind of stress is also called 'sentence stress' and is different from 'word stress' (mentioned under *Pronunciation* above). Word stress relates to stressed *syllables* in a *word*, while sentence stress relates to stressed *words* in a *sentence*. Adding emphasis to key words in your talk will make it easier for the audience to follow you presentation as they are more likely to understand which are your main points. In general, function words and phrases (such as 'What I want to talk about today' and 'Let's turn now to the next section') should be said more quickly, while content words (the ones which carry meaning) need to be spoken more slowly. The key words in your speech will all be content words.

> **In short**
> Focus on *content* words, and add **emphasis** by:
> - saying the words more slowly;
> - saying the words more loudly;
> - pausing briefly before and after the word.

# Checklist

Below is a checklist for delivery. Ask a peer to use it to assess you when you practise. (This is a difficult area to self-assess, though you could do this if you are able to video yourself or record your voice, e.g. on a mobile phone.)

| Area | Item | OK? | Comments |
|---|---|---|---|
| **Pace** | The pace is a little slower than normal speed. | | |
| **Pronunciation** | Key words are pronounced correctly. | | |
| **Volume** | The volume is appropriate. | | |
| | The speaker is audible from the back of the room. | | |
| **Emphasis** | Stress is used to emphasise key words or ideas. | | |
| | The speaker adds stress by saying the word more loudly, more slowly, and by pausing before or after the word. | | |
| | The speaker stresses the right kind of words (content words/key words). | | |

Unit 6: **Delivery**

# Exercises

## Exercise 1: **Comprehension**

Answer the following questions about this unit. Either do this after reading the unit, or make notes first then use your notes to answer the questions.

1  What is the best way to improve *delivery*? [Hint: answer this question using *one word*!]
   _____

2  What are the four elements of effective *delivery* given in this unit?
   - 
   - 
   - 
   - 

3  Why is it important to speak more slowly than usual when giving a presentation?
   _____
   _____

4  Complete this general rule: *The larger the audience, the* _____

5  In what way is pronunciation for a presentation different from ordinary speech?
   _____
   _____

6  Why is *too loud* better than *too quiet*?
   _____
   _____

7  Give three possible sources of noise in a presentation, and ways to reduce them.

| Source of noise | Way to reduce it |
| --- | --- |
|  |  |
|  |  |
|  |  |

79

# EAP Foundation: Academic Presentations

8 What is the difference between 'sentence stress' and 'word stress'?
_____
_____

9 What type of words should be emphasised?
_____
_____

10 How do you add *emphasis* to a word?
- 
- 
- 

## Exercise 2: **Emphasis**

Study the following presentation introduction from Unit 2, Exercise 2 again. <u>Underline</u> all the words which you think should be stressed.

> Let me begin by asking you a question: How do you prefer to learn? Perhaps you prefer to be in a group, or perhaps you study better on your own. Perhaps you learn best by listening, or perhaps you remember information better if you see it. Maybe you like to snack while you learn, have music on, and so on and so forth. These differences in the way we like to learn are called learning styles, and understanding your own preferences can be an important first step in improving how you study. Good afternoon everyone. I'm Steven Kirby, from the department of Educational Psychology, and what I want to look at today is learning styles, focusing on two of the main models of learning style used in educational contexts. I'll begin by giving a historical overview of learning styles, then give details about the two main models, namely the VAK model and the Dunn and Dunn model. I'll conclude by considering how learning styles can improve study. My aim today is to get you thinking about your own learning style and how you can use it to improve your learning. My presentation should last around twelve minutes. You may have some questions as we go along, but I'd be grateful if you could wait until the end of my presentation before you ask them.

Now read it aloud, paying attention to the stressed words. If possible, ask a partner to ==highlight== words which are stressed, and afterwards compare. Do your underlining and your partner's highlighting match up? Could your partner hear the words you wanted to stress?

# Unit 6: **Delivery**

## Exercise 3: **Pronunciation**

Use the table below to make a list of some of the key words you plan to use in your speech (continue on another sheet if necessary). Record their pronunciation (use a dictionary or teacher to help). Remember to make a note of the word stress as well. You should categorise them by part of speech (this will help you to not only say them correctly, but hopefully use them correctly). If possible, *try to check* by reading the words to your teacher. The words across a line do not need to be related (see the four example words, which have been recorded in different ways).

| Nouns | Verbs | Adj/Adv | Other e.g. phrases |
|---|---|---|---|
| o ooOo<br>pronunciation | emphasise<br>/ˈem.fə.saɪz/ | o Ooo o<br>spon-ta-ne-ous | place EMphasis on<br>/ə/ |
|  |  |  |  |
|  |  |  |  |
|  |  |  |  |
|  |  |  |  |
|  |  |  |  |
|  |  |  |  |

# EAP Foundation: Academic Presentations

## Exercise 4: **Practice**

Practise giving your presentation, using the checklist in this unit to get feedback, either by assessing yourself or asking a peer to help you. It is enough to practise just one section, for example the Introduction, in order to get feedback. If you do not have a presentation to work on, you can use the outline presentation in *Appendix 6: Presentation Outline*.

## Exercise 5: **Progress check**

**First**, look back at *Exercise 4: Preparation* in Unit 1. Find any questions you highlighted because you could not answer them before. Can you answer any of these questions now? If so, record the answer.

**Then**, return to *Exercise 5: Planning your presentation* in Unit 1. Which stage should you be at now? Are you on track? Do you need to adjust the timing? Make a note of your progress (e.g. any stages which are now 'Started' or 'Complete') in the 'Progress' column.

# Appendices

# Appendix 1: Accessing Online Resources

## About online resources

There are additional online resources for each unit. These resources include worksheets, copies of checklists, teaching tips, lesson plans and mp3 recordings (for books in the speaking and listening series). These resources are available free of charge. All you need is an access code (see below).

## How to access online resources

Follow these steps to access the resources.
1) Go to http://www.evidentpress.com/resources/.
2) To access the resources, you will first need to register. If you have already done this, skip to step 3). If not, click on **Register** and follow the onscreen instructions, which will require you to enter a username, your first name, last name, email address and password.
3) Use your login details to log in to the site. This will take you to your **Resources** page. This screen will tell you which books you already have access to, if any.
4) Click on the button **Add Resources**. Enter the access code to gain access to the resources. The code for *EAP Foundation: Academic Presentations* is shown below.

### ACCESS CODE: 7Gh9vMm

You will only need to enter this code once. In future when you log in, the resources for this book will automatically show up.

If you follow the above steps, you should be able to access all the resources for the book. If you have any difficulty entering the code, registering or logging in, please contact Evident Press by using the form on the Evident Press contact page, or directly at contact@evidentpress.com.

# Appendix 2: Answers to exercises

## Unit 1

### Unit 1, Exercise 1: Comprehension

1. What are the six key areas to consider when preparing a presentation? Write them below, then match each one to the appropriate *wh-* question word. An example has been done.
   - audience – *who*
   - purpose – *why*
   - tone – *how*
   - venue – *where*
   - timing – *when*
   - content – *what*

2. Write down *two* questions you can ask about the audience.
   *See unit for questions.*

3. Why is the purpose 'To get a high score!' not an appropriate one?
   This is the purpose *in relation to you*, not the audience.

4. The *general* purpose of a presentation is usually expressed using a verb. Write down *five* such verbs.
   - to inform
   - to persuade
   - to instruct
   - to motivate
   - to entertain

5. Which of the purposes in question 4 above are most suited to *academic* presentations?
   *The purposes* to inform *and* to persuade *are most common in academic presentations.* To instruct *is also possible, though less likely. The other two are uncommon in academic presentations.*

6. How is the tone of an academic presentation *similar to* academic writing? How is it *different*?
   - Similar – *language*
   - Different – *presence, images*

7. What is a 'back-up plan', and why is it important to have one for your presentation?
   A plan of what you will do if things go wrong. It is important for a presentation because there are many things which could go wrong (broken computer, broken memory stick, etc.), so you should anticipate problems and prepare for them.

# EAP Foundation: Academic Presentations

**8** Why might the time of day you give your presentation be important?
It could affect your approach and content. E.g. if you are presenting after lunch, the audience might be sleepy, so you might want to do something to wake them up.

**9** How is the content of an *informational* presentation different from a *persuasive* one?
- Informational presentation   contains strongest information and data
- Persuasive presentation   contains convincing and logical arguments and evidence

**10** Complete the stages in *planning a presentation* by using words from the box to fill the gaps.

1. Understand the task
2. Prepare for the task
3. Research the topic
4. Select content
5. Make visual aids
6. Practise
7. Make improvements
8. Continue to practise
9. Make final improvements
10. Make final arrangements
11. Give presentation
12. Reflect on performance

# Appendices

## Unit 1, Exercise 2: **Solving Common Problems**

| Problem | Area | Possible solution(s) – *when preparing* |
|---|---|---|
| 1. The projector in the room does not work. | Venue | - Prepare handouts for the audience.<br>- Be ready to give a presentation *without* PPT. |
| 2. The computer in the room has an older version of Microsoft Office and your PowerPoint does not display properly. | Venue | - Check the equipment before the presentation.<br>- Ask if you can bring your own laptop to use in the presentation.<br>- Make sure you have a back-up e.g. handouts or PDF version of your PPT. |
| 3. The presentation is too technical and the audience cannot follow the main points. | Audience | - Find out who your audience will be and what they already know about the topic. |
| 4. The audience grows bored with the presentation and at the end, someone ask what it was about. | Purpose | - Make sure you have a clear purpose for your presentation (*general* purpose and *specific* purpose). |
| 5. You have prepared a 30 minute presentation, but are told you can only talk for ten. | Timing | - Check how long your presentation should be before you begin preparing the content. |
| 6. You have prepared ten handouts for the audience, but when you get to the room you find there are 50 people. | Audience | - Check how many people will be in the audience.<br>- Prepare some extra copies of the handout, in case more people attend. |
| 7. You prepared a ten minute presentation, but after fifteen minutes you are only halfway through and are told to stop. | Content | - Do not include too much.<br>- Practise your presentation to see how long it will take. |
| 8. You try to make your presentation humorous by including several jokes, but no one laughs. | Tone | - Make sure the tone relates to the audience and purpose.<br>- Be careful of telling jokes! If the audience does not laugh, you will only feel more nervous. |

# EAP Foundation: Academic Presentations

## Unit 1, Exercise 3: **General and Specific Purpose**

| Type | General Purpose |
|---|---|
| informational | to inform |
| persuasive | to persuade |
| instructional | to instruct |
| motivational | to motivate |
| entertaining | to entertain |

| Specific Purpose Examples | Type |
|---|---|
| a) The purpose of my presentation is to inform you of the different types of purpose a presentation can have. | informational |
| b) What I want to do today is show why informational presentations are better than instructional ones. | persuasive |
| c) My purpose today is to outline simple ways you can exercise while at work, and, hopefully, get you exercising more! | motivational |
| d) My purpose this afternoon is to show you how to give a terrible presentation! | humorous |
| e) My purpose today is to report on how often Business students use persuasive presentations. | informational |
| f) My purpose today is to demonstrate how to give an effective presentation. | instructional |
| g) I'm here today to introduce the findings of our research project on eating habits in the over-sixties. | informational |
| h) What I'm going to do this morning is explain why global warming is the most significant threat to our planet today. | persuasive |

Language notes
- The verbs 'to inform', 'to report' and 'to introduce' suggest informational *presentations*.
- The phrases 'show why' and 'explain why' indicate the speaker will give reasons to support their opinion, which suggest persuasive *presentations*.
- The verb 'to demonstrate (how to do sth)' suggests an instructional *presentation*. Other examples are 'to show you (how)' or 'to explain (how)'.
- The phrase 'get you exercising more' suggests the speaker wants to encourage the audience to take action, which would make it a motivational *presentation*.
- There is no special language for a humorous presentation. The topic suggests it will be humorous (no one wants to learn how to give a bad presentation!).

Appendices

# Unit 2

## Unit 2, Exercise 1: **Comprehension**

1 Put the following parts of a presentation Introduction into the order they *usually* occur. An example has been done for you.

   **a)** arouse interest
   **b)** greet audience
   **c)** introduce yourself
   **d)** state topic and focus
   **e)** state purpose
   **f)** give structure
   **g)** give timing
   **h)** give information about Q&A

2 What is a 'hook' and why might it be best to start with this?

   A hook is something which arouses the audience's interest at the start of a presentation. Although not essential for an academic presentation, it is useful to start with a hook because the audience will be more likely to pay attention from the start, which will help you to achieve your aim.

3 Give three different types of 'hook' which can be used in presentations.
   *Any three of the following:*
   - *story*
   - *video/graphic*
   - *humorous anecdote*
   - *rhetorical question*
   - *interesting or controversial statement*

4 Some writers describe the outline of a presentation in this way: *Tell them what you are going to tell them; tell them; then tell them what you told them.* What do you think this means? Why might it be good advice?
   'Tell them what you are going to tell them' refers to stating the topic and focus and giving the outline in the Introduction. 'Tell them' refers to the information in the Main Body. 'Tell them what you told them' refers to the summary in the Conclusion. This is good advice because it ensures your main points are crystal clear. Remember that listening is a difficult skill, and repetition will help the audience remember.

# EAP Foundation: Academic Presentations

**5** What are the elements of an effective conclusion?
*A conclusion should contain the following:*
- *a brief summary of the major points;*
- *a final 'take-away' message;*
- *a 'thank you' message for the audience;*
- *an invitation to ask questions (the Q&A).*

**6** What is a 'take-away' message and why is it important?
It is the one main idea that you want the audience to remember (or 'take away') from the presentation.

**7** In what way is the Q&A different from the rest of the presentation?
It is two-way rather than one way traffic (i.e. it is *interactive*). It is also different because you cannot rehearse it (though you can anticipate questions as you prepare).

**8** What are the four different types of Q&A question given in this unit?
- clarification
- expansion
- challenge
- off-topic

## Unit 2, Exercise 2: Identifying Parts of an Introduction

Let me begin by asking you a question: How do you prefer to learn? Perhaps you prefer to be in a group, or perhaps you study better on your own. Perhaps you learn best by listening, or perhaps you remember information better if you see it. Maybe you like to snack while you learn, have music on, and so on and so forth. These differences in the way we like to learn are called learning styles, and understanding your own preferences can be an important first step in improving how you study. — *arouse interest*

Good afternoon everyone. — *greet the audience*

I'm Steven Kirby, from the department of Educational Psychology, — *introduce yourself*

and what I want to look at today is learning styles, focusing on — *state the topic and focus*

two of the main models of learning style used in educational contexts.

I'll begin by giving a historical overview of learning styles, then give details about the two main models, namely the VAK model and the Dunn and Dunn model. I'll conclude by considering how learning styles can improve study. — *outline the structure*

My aim today is to get you thinking about your own learning style and how you can use it to improve your learning. — *state the purpose*

My presentation should last around twelve minutes. — *give timing*

You may have some questions as we go along, but I'd be grateful if you could wait until the end of my presentation before you ask them. — *say when you will answer questions*

## Unit 2, Exercise 3: **Identifying Content of a Presentation**

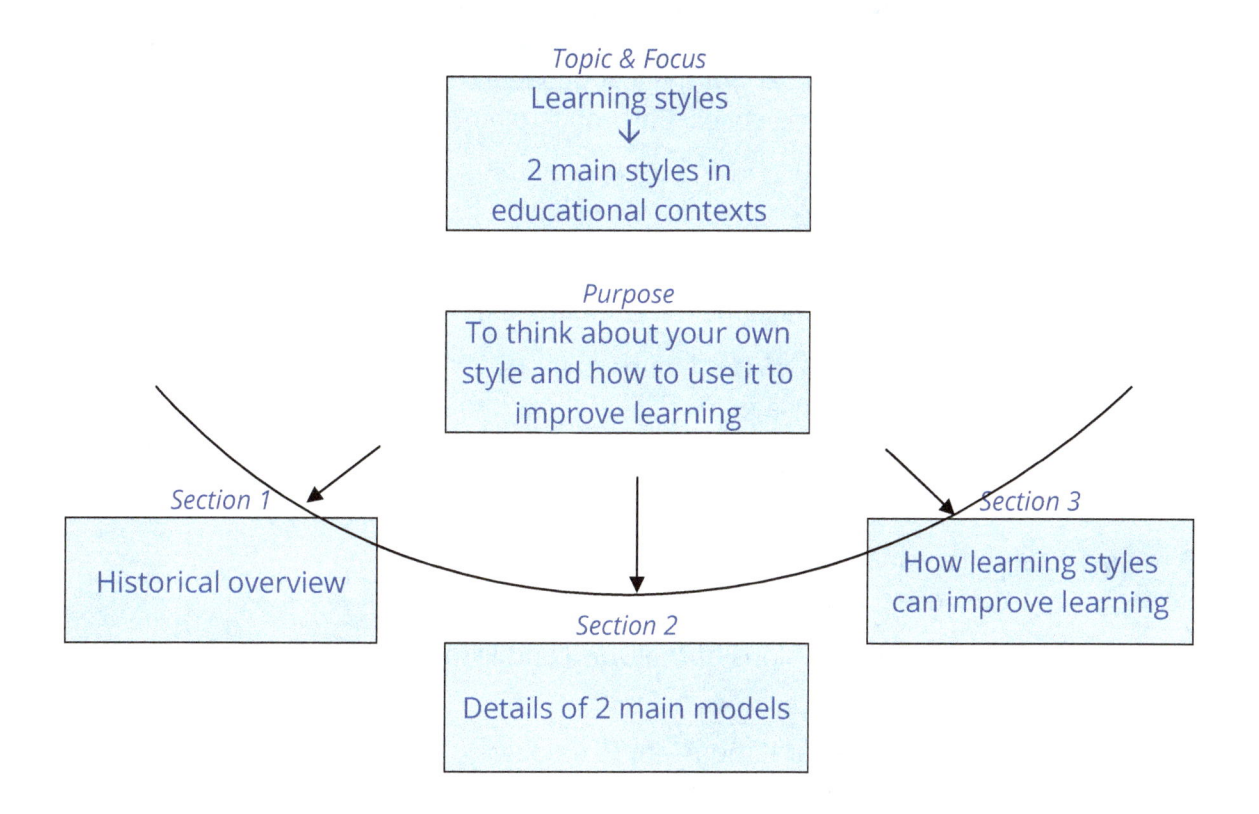

*Topic & Focus*
Learning styles
↓
2 main styles in educational contexts

*Purpose*
To think about your own style and how to use it to improve learning

*Section 1*
Historical overview

*Section 2*
Details of 2 main models

*Section 3*
How learning styles can improve learning

# EAP Foundation: Academic Presentations

## Unit 2, Exercise 4: **Q&A Question Types**

| Question | Type |
|---|---|
| I didn't quite get what you said about the link between the Kolb learning cycle and learning styles. Can you explain? | Clarification |
| Are you sure that the Dunn and Dunn model is commonly used in teacher training in the USA? | Challenge |
| You talked about there being over 70 different models of learning styles. Can you give us some more examples? | Expansion |
| You talked about the VAK model, but I didn't quite catch what the letter K was for. Can tell us again? | Clarification |
| Why do you think students today are so bad at completing their homework? | Off-topic |
| You've presented these styles as fact, but isn't it true that there is very little research to support them? | Challenge |
| Can you tell us the five dimensions of the Dunn and Dunn model again? | Clarification |
| You said that learning styles are important in teacher training courses. Where did you do your teacher training? | Off-topic |
| You gave examples of how *visual* learners can improve their study. Could you give some more examples? | Expansion |
| Can you go over the history of learning styles one more time? | Clarification |

# Appendices

# Unit 3

## Unit 3, Exercise 1: **Comprehension**

1 What are 'signpost' phrases?
   Phrases which signpost (i.e. signal) the direction of your talk.

2 How many of the phrases in this unit do you need to learn?
   At least one for each function (probably more for referring to visuals and transitions between sections, as you will do these more than once in a presentation).

3 Give two phrases for *stating the topic and focus*. Which *one* of these do you think you might use in your presentation?
   *See unit for phrases. Which one you prefer depends on you!*

4 Give two phrases for *stating the purpose*. Which *one* of these do you think you might use in your presentation?
   *See unit for phrases. Which one you prefer depends on you!*

5 What is the function of each of the following phrases?
   - Sorry about this. I'll have it fixed in just a second.  Recover from technical problems
   - Anyway, as I was saying…  Resume (after digression etc.)
   - Let me give you an example…  Give examples
   - So far, I've presented…  Summarise

6 In which section would you normally use/hear these phrases?
   - That's a great question.  Q&A
   - Thank you very much.  Conclusion
   - At the end of my talk, there will be a chance to ask questions  Introduction
   - Does that answer your question?  Q&A

93

# EAP Foundation: Academic Presentations

## Unit 3, Exercise 2: **Language for Introductions**

a)

| Language function | Corrected sentence |
|---|---|
| Introduce yourself | My name <u>are</u>... *(is)* |
| State topic/focus | What I want to talk ^ today is... *(about)* |
| State the purpose | The purpose of my presentation is ^ give an overview of... *(to)* |
| Arouse interest | Let me begin by <u>ask</u> you a question. *(asking)* |
| Give structure | This talk <u>divides</u> into three main parts. *(is divided)* |
| Give timing | My presentation <u>takes</u> about 15 minutes. *(will take)* |
| Handle questions | I'll be happy to answer <u>some</u> questions you have at the end of my presentation *(any)* |

b)

| Language function | Completed sentence |
|---|---|
| Greet audience | Good <u>morning/afternoon/day</u>, everyone. |
| State the purpose | My <u>aim/purpose/objective</u> today is to... |
| Give structure | To <u>begin/start</u> with, I'd like to look at... |
| Give structure | My fourth <u>point</u> will be about... |
| Give structure | Finally, I'll be <u>looking</u> at... |

# Appendices

## Unit 3, Exercise 3: Language for Main Body

*The order is **C-B-A**. All phrases are **transition** phrases except for the first one ('Having looked at...') which is used to **summarise** the preceding section.*

**A** This particular theory of learning styles is especially common in training courses in the USA. **//**<u>Having looked at</u> the two main styles, <u>I'd like to move on to my final area, which is</u> considering how these styles can be used to improve your own learning. As we have seen, each of us prefers to learn in a different way, and if we can be more aware of *how* we prefer to learn…

**B** …which led to interest in different styles. Some studies suggest there are over 70 such styles in total. **//**<u>Right, let's now move on now to the second area, which is</u> a detailed look at the two main models of learning styles, beginning with the VAK model. This model is probably the most well-known…

**C** … please feel free to ask me at the end. **//**<u>OK, so let me begin by talking a little about</u> the history of learning styles. Learning styles first became prominent in the field of education in the mid-1970s…

## Unit 3, Exercise 4: Language for Transitions and Visuals

| | | | | |
|---|---|---|---|---|
| a | This leads me to | iv | my next point… | (T) |
| b | As you | viii | can see here… | (V) |
| c | Here | ix | we can see… | (V) |
| d | I'd now like to move | vii | on to… | (T) |
| e | This table | vi | shows… | (V) |
| f | Let me | ii | show you… | (V) |
| g | Let's now | i | turn to… | (T) |
| h | I now want | v | to go on to… | (T) |
| i | I'd like you to | iii | look at this. | (V) |

## Unit 3, Exercise 5: Language for Conclusions

| Language function | Completed sentence |
|---|---|
| Give summary | So, to <u>conclude/sum up</u>… |
| Give 'take-away' message | Let me <u>finish/end</u> by saying… |
| Thank audience | Thank you for your <u>attention/time</u>. |
| Invite questions | If you have any <u>questions</u> I'll be happy to answer them now. |

# Unit 4

## Unit 4, Exercise 1: **Comprehension**

1 The following chart summarises the information for each type of visual aid. Use the information in the unit to complete the gaps.

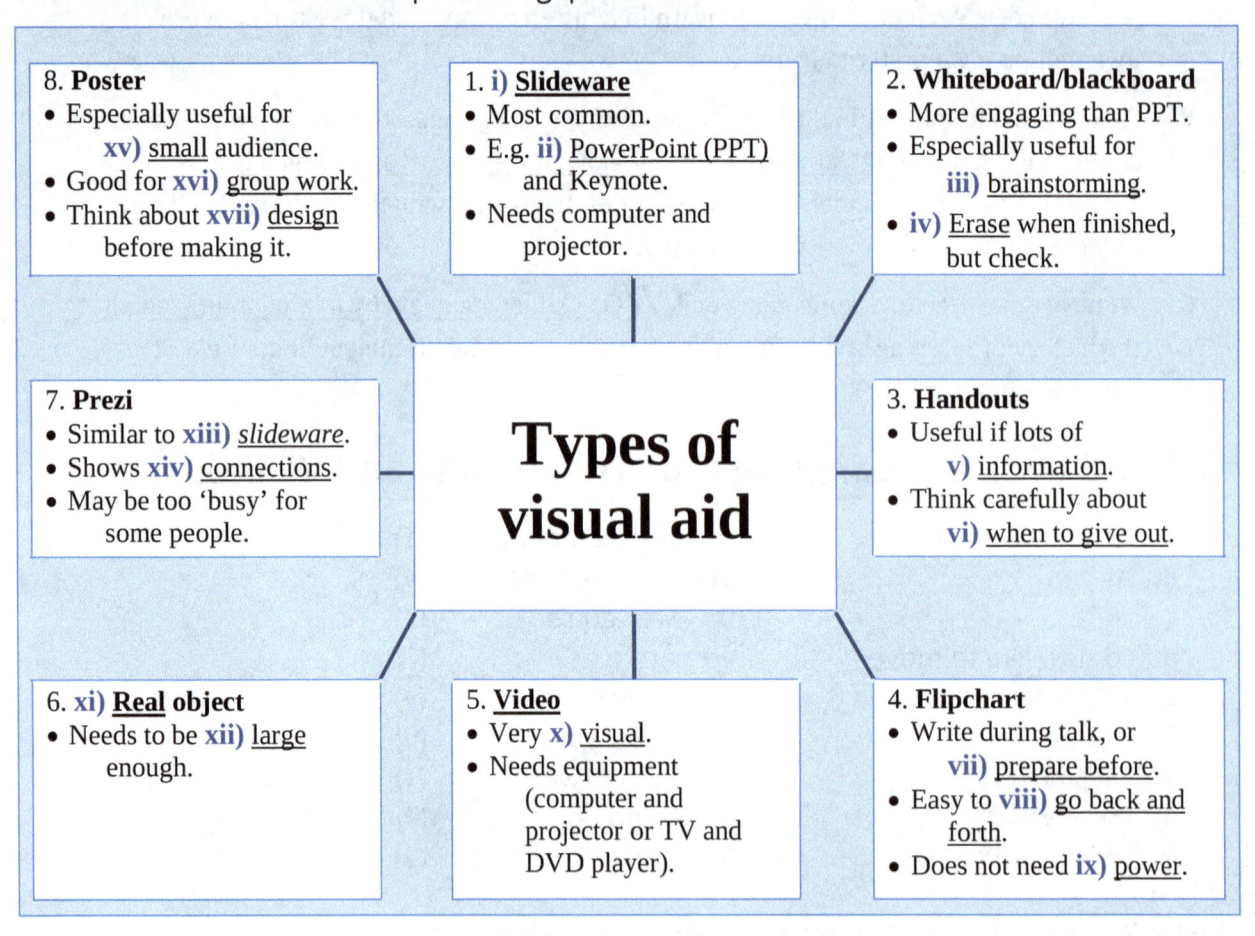

**Types of visual aid**

**8. Poster**
- Especially useful for **xv)** small audience.
- Good for **xvi)** group work.
- Think about **xvii)** design before making it.

**1. i)** Slideware
- Most common.
- E.g. **ii)** PowerPoint (PPT) and Keynote.
- Needs computer and projector.

**2. Whiteboard/blackboard**
- More engaging than PPT.
- Especially useful for **iii)** brainstorming.
- **iv)** Erase when finished, but check.

**7. Prezi**
- Similar to **xiii)** slideware.
- Shows **xiv)** connections.
- May be too 'busy' for some people.

**3. Handouts**
- Useful if lots of **v)** information.
- Think carefully about **vi)** when to give out.

**6. xi)** Real object
- Needs to be **xii)** large enough.

**5.** Video
- Very **x)** visual.
- Needs equipment (computer and projector or TV and DVD player).

**4. Flipchart**
- Write during talk, or **vii)** prepare before.
- Easy to **viii)** go back and forth.
- Does not need **ix)** power.

# Appendices

**2** Match the following types of information with the best way to present each one.

| Type of information | Best way to present it |
| --- | --- |
| Information on the main factors of the US economy compared to those of the Indian economy. | table |
| A demonstration of how to conduct a simple laboratory experiment. | diagram |
| Information on the factors which contribute to GDP. | text |
| Month-by-month data on the US dollar-UK pound exchange rate from 2015 to 2017. | graph |
| An example of the damage suffered by buildings in Dresden during aerial bombings in WWII. | photograph |
| The percentage of students who prefer different types of hobby (totalling 100%). | pie chart |
| A comparison of total revenue from imports (in US$) for China and Japan, in 2000, 2005, 2010 and 2015. | bar chart |

**3** Why is the colour of background and lettering of a visual aid important?
It needs to be *visual*. If background and lettering are both very dark (or both very light) the information might be difficult to see.

**4** Why might the size of text in a visual be an issue?
Small text might not be visible from the back of the room.

**5** What is the recommended size of text for PPT?
Font size 24 or above is recommended.

**6** Why should you include a visual (e.g. PPT slide) showing the structure, and another giving a summary?
It will 'aid' your presentation by helping the audience understand the main points.

**7** Why might having too much text in your visual be a problem?
The audience may spend too much time reading instead of listening.

**8** What is the name of the 'rule' related to the amount of text in the visual?
The rule is the six-by-six rule.

**9** What is wrong with using a cute (but unrelated) picture in your presentation?
It does not add to the overall message.

**10** What does *consistency* mean in relation to visual aids?
It refers to two things. First, make sure PowerPoint slides have a parallel structure (e.g. all noun phrases). Second, if you are working as part of a group, make sure all group members use the same format for visuals (e.g. PPT).

# EAP Foundation: Academic Presentations

## Unit 4, Exercise 2: **Assessing Risk**

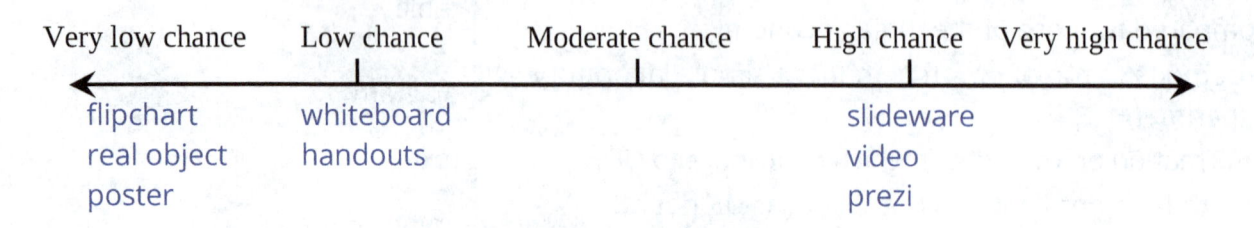

Very low chance — Low chance — Moderate chance — High chance — Very high chance

- flipchart (Very low chance)
- real object (Very low chance)
- poster (Very low chance)
- whiteboard (Low chance)
- handouts (Low chance)
- slideware (High chance)
- video (High chance)
- prezi (High chance)

## Unit 4, Exercise 3: **Creating PowerPoint slides**

*The following are possible answers. The information is summarised, so not everything is included. Both use parallel structure (noun phrases for GDP, verb phrases for GNP). Neither follow the 6-by-6 rule (GDP has 7 lines, max 7 words, GNP has 8 lines max 7 words).*

**GDP**

- Gross Domestic Product
- Measure of nation's overall economy
- Value of all final goods and services
- Measurement for a given year
- Two ways to measure:
    1. total value of purchases
    2. total value of production

**GNP**

- Means 'Gross National Product'
- Is similar to GDP
- Adds what is produced by businesses abroad
- Subtracts payments sent to other countries
- Is close to GDP for some countries
    - e.g. USA (within 0.2%)
- Is very different for some countries
    - e.g. many people working abroad

# Appendices

## Unit 5

### Unit 5, Exercise 1: **Comprehension**

1 Why might your body's message be less clear to you than your verbal message?
<u>Because you cannot see your body language, so you do not know what your body is 'saying' (but you can hear your voice and you know what your words mean).</u>

2 Correct this sentence: *Good speakers* ~~are~~ *appear* *confident.*

3 How should you *position* yourself when giving a presentation?
<u>Face the audience.</u>

4 What should you do if you need to look at the screen?
<u>Stop talking, look at the screen, then face the audience again when you continue to speak.</u>

5 What are the benefits of good *posture*?
<u>It will help you to look better, feel better and sound better.</u>

6 Why is *movement* important during a presentation?
<u>It conveys energy to the audience (audience members respond best to presenters who are energetic).</u>

7 What types of *movement* should you be aware of during a presentation?
- *body*
- *face and head*
- *hands*

8 What is the problem with *too much* movement?
<u>It can be distracting.</u>

9 What is 'gestural vocabulary'? Give examples.
<u>Gestural vocabulary is the use of hands to express something specific, and is generally the same in all languages. Examples are counting, expressing something big (with hands held wide) or something small (hands held together).</u>

10 Why is *eye contact* important?
*Eye contact is important for the following reasons:*
- *it creates a relationship between the speaker and the audience;*
- *it encourages the audience to listen;*
- *it helps the speaker to relax;*
- *it helps the speaker understand if the audience is following.*

99

# EAP Foundation: Academic Presentations

## Unit 5, Exercise 2: **Hand Movement**

*The underlined words are ones which could be emphasised or clarified with hand gestures, though it is unlikely you would use hand gestures for all of them.*

      *(use hand to signal 'three')*                           *(use hand to signal 'one')*
There are <u>three</u> types of movement to consider during a presentation. The <u>first</u> is movement

    *(use hands to indicate your 'body')*
of your <u>body</u>. Too much body movement can be distracting, so make sure not to move

        *(use hand to signal 'two')*       *(use hand to indicate your 'face/head')*
around too much. The <u>second</u> type of movement is movement of your <u>face or head</u>. These

are very expressive parts of your body, and you should take care to ensure that your facial

                    *(use hand to signal 'three')*
expressions and head movements are positive. The <u>third</u> and final type of movement to

        *(use hands to indicate your 'hands'!)*      *(use hands for emphasis)*
consider is movement of your <u>hands</u>. This type of movement can have a <u>big</u> effect on

whether you look confident or not.

# Appendices

# Unit 6

## Unit 6, Exercise 1: **Comprehension**

1. What is the best way to improve *delivery*? [Hint: answer this question using *one word*!]
   Practise

2. What are the four elements of effective *delivery* given in this unit?
   - *pace*
   - *pronunciation*
   - *volume*
   - *emphasis*

3. Why is it important to speak more slowly than usual when giving a presentation?
   *It is important to speak more slowly for the following reasons:*
   - *the audience needs time to hear and understand the main points*
   - *it can help you calm your nerves*
   - *it can help you focus on pronunciation*

4. Complete this general rule: The larger the audience, the more slowly you need to speak.

5. In what way is pronunciation for a presentation different from ordinary speech?
   It is not! But because a presentation is rehearsed (not spontaneous) you have a chance to identify and practise the pronunciation of keys words.

6. Why is *too loud* better than *too quiet*?
   Although it is annoying, the audience can still hear your main points.

7. Give three possible sources of noise in a presentation, and ways to reduce them.

   | Source of noise | Way to reduce it |
   | --- | --- |
   | Outside (through open door/window) | Close door/windows |
   | Inside (audience talking) | Ask audience members to keep quiet |
   | Yourself (nervous tapping of pen) | Watch out for your nervous noises! |

8. What is the difference between 'sentence stress' and 'word stress'?
   Sentence stress relates to *words* in a *sentence* which are stressed.
   Word stress relates to *syllables* in a *word* which are stressed.

9. What type of words should be emphasised?
   Content words (including key words)

10. How do you add *emphasis* to a word?
    - *Say it more slowly*
    - *Say it more loudly*
    - *Pause (before/after the word)*

# EAP Foundation: Academic Presentations

## Unit 6, Exercise 2: **Emphasis**

*The following are some possible words which could be stressed. These are mostly key words in the talk, and are not all of the content words.*

Let me begin by asking you a question: <u>How</u> do you prefer to <u>learn</u>? Perhaps you prefer to be in a <u>group</u>, or perhaps you study better <u>on your own</u>. Perhaps you learn best by <u>listening</u>, or perhaps you remember information better if you <u>see</u> it. Maybe you like to <u>snack</u> while you learn, have <u>music</u> on, and so on and so forth. These <u>differences</u> the way we like to learn are called <u>learning styles</u>, and understanding your <u>own</u> preferences can be an <u>important first step</u> in <u>improving</u> how you study. Good afternoon everyone. I'm <u>Steven Kirby</u>, from the department of <u>Educational Psychology</u>, and what I want to look at today is <u>learning styles</u>, focusing on <u>two</u> of the <u>main</u> models of learning style used in <u>educational contexts</u>. I'll begin by giving a <u>historical overview</u> of learning styles, then give details about the <u>two main models</u>, namely the <u>VAK</u> model and the <u>Dunn and Dunn</u> model. I'll conclude by considering <u>how</u> learning styles can <u>improve study</u>. My <u>aim</u> today is to get you <u>thinking</u> about your <u>own learning style</u> and how you can use it to <u>improve</u> your <u>learning</u>. My presentation should last around <u>twelve</u> minutes. You may have some questions as we go along, but I'd be grateful if you could wait until the <u>end</u> of my presentation before you ask them.

*See the online resources for a recording of this passage* (**see** *Appendix 1*). *Listen to check the emphasised words.*

# Appendix 3: **Presentation topics**

The following presentation topics can be used to help practise all elements of this book. They are especially useful if you have no assessed presentation to work on, or if you want to work through the book using a different task. The topics have been chosen to match ones used throughout the EAP Foundation series. They relate to a range of common academic disciplines, yet at the same time are focused on topics of general interest. All relate to data in *Appendix 4: Data for Visual Aids*.

## Topic 1: Economics

| Topic area | Economics > Macroeconomics |
|---|---|
| **Task** | Examine the current GDP of a given country. |
| **Task notes** | In order to understand the current GDP of a country, you will need to make comparisons. This could be:<br>• over time, e.g. how GDP has changed from the past to now;<br>• in relation to other countries, e.g. by looking at how GDP for your chosen country compares to other countries or to the world figure. |
| **Additional notes** | If you tackle the task in a simple way, for example over the course of one or two lessons, the data in *Appendix 4: Data for Visual Aids* should be enough. You may want to focus on the USA, as additional information is given for that country, though this is not essential. If you wish to tackle the task in a more extended fashion, you will probably want to find out more about the following:<br>• the factors which contribute to GDP (*Economic theory*);<br>• background information for your chosen country, e.g. demographics, politics, location, size, political situation (*for background information*);<br>• economic information for your chosen country, e.g. main industries, economy (*to understand reasons for size of GDP*). |
| **Resources** | 1) See *Appendix 4: Presentation Data (Economics data)* for data on GDP.<br>2) See *Unit 4: Visual Aids*, Exercise 4 for information on GDP.<br>3) Log in to the resources page of Evident Press website to access additional resources related to this topic, including links to background information and more detailed GDP data. See *Appendix 1: Accessing Online Resources* for instructions. |

# Topic 2: Health

| | |
|---|---|
| **Topic area** | Medical Sciences > Health |
| **Task** | Obesity is an increasing but preventable problem in many countries. |
| **Task notes** | In order to answer this task, you will need to:<br>• look at current obesity data for different countries (especially those where obesity levels are high);<br>• examine how obesity levels in different countries have increased over time;<br>• understand the adverse health effects to individuals of obesity (e.g. diabetes);<br>• understand the causes of obesity and possible solutions (this relates to 'preventable'). |
| **Additional notes** | If you tackle the task in a simple way, for example over the course of one or two lessons, the data in *Appendix 4: Data for Visual Aids* should be enough. You may want to use the USA as an example country with an obesity problem, as additional information is given for that country, though this is not essential. If you wish to tackle the task in a more extended fashion, you will probably want to do more research. Possible areas to find out more about are:<br>• physical effects of obesity (besides diabetes);<br>• economic effects of obesity (how does an obese workforce affect the economy?);<br>• further details on the causes of obesity (e.g. types of food consumed, sedentary lifestyles);<br>• further solutions to obesity (e.g. government action such as 'sugar tax'). |
| **Resources** | 1) See *Appendix 4: Presentation Data (Health data)* for data on obesity.<br>2) Log in to the resources page of Evident Press website to access additional resources related to this topic, including links to background information and more detailed obesity data. See *Appendix 1: Accessing Online Resources* for instructions. |

# Appendices

# Topic 3: Sociology

| Topic area | Sociology >Demographics |
|---|---|
| **Task** | Examine the demographic situation of a given country. |
| **Task notes** | In order to understand the demographic situation of a country, you will need to look at various factors, such as:<br>• current population change, the equation for which is:<br>    Fertility rate – Mortality rate + Net Migration<br>    (be careful if Net Migration is negative, this will *reduce* the figure);<br>• population change over time;<br>• demographic information in relation to other countries, e.g. fertility rate, mortality rate, migration rate and population size for your chosen country compared to other countries. |
| **Additional notes** | If you tackle the task in a simple way, for example over the course of one or two lessons, the data in *Appendix 4: Data for Visual Aids* should be enough. If you wish to tackle the task in a more extended fashion, you will probably want to do more research and find out more about the following:<br>• the population data for different age ranges (e.g. 0-4, 5-9, and so on);<br>• population of males compared to females, overall or for different age ranges (the later would allow you to draw a *population pyramid*);<br>• reasons for changes in population (better healthcare, education, etc.). |
| **Resources** | 1) See *Appendix 4: Presentation Data* for.<br>2) Log in to the resources page of Evident Press website to access additional resources related to this topic, including links to background information and more detailed GDP data. See *Appendix 1: Accessing Online Resources* for instructions. |

-- For further tasks (and data), see the online resources. --

# Appendix 4: Data for visual aids

The data on the following pages can be used to create visual aids for use in practice presentations. The data match topics found in *Appendix 3: Presentation Topics*. Exercise 4 in *Unit 4: Visual Aids* also uses these data.

## Economics data

The following table shows contributors to **GDP for the USA** in 2016 Q4 (fourth quarter), in billions of dollars. Details are shown for *Personal consumption*. Total GDP: **$18,905.6 billion**.

| Contributor | Amount | Percent |
|---|---|---|
| **Personal consumption** | **13056.9** | **69%** |
| Goods | 4195.9 | |
| Durable goods | 1440.2 | |
| Motor vehicles and parts | 500 | |
| Furnishings and durable household equipment | 328.2 | |
| Recreational goods and vehicles | 389.2 | |
| Other durable goods | 222.8 | |
| Nondurable goods | 2755.7 | |
| Food and beverages | 922.3 | |
| Clothing and footwear | 395.3 | |
| Gasoline and other energy goods | 294 | |
| Other nondurable goods | 1144.1 | |
| Services | 8861 | |
| Housing and utilities | 2369.9 | |
| Health care | 2208 | |
| Transportation services | 398.4 | |
| Recreation services | 501.5 | |
| Food services and accommodations | 860.4 | |
| Financial services and insurance | 1007.1 | |
| Other services | 1515.6 | |
| **Private domestic investment** | **3126.2** | **17%** |
| **Exports** | **2241.5** | **12%** |
| **Imports** | **-2805.8** | **-15%** |
| **Government spending and investment** | **3286.8** | **17%** |

Source: U.S. Bureau of Economic Analysis, "Table 1.2.5. Gross Domestic Product by Major Type of Product," https://bea.gov/iTable/index.cfm (accessed 27 December, 2017).

# Economics data (cont'd)

The following table shows **GDP** for different countries, covering six different years, each a decade apart. Figures are per capita, in US$. World data are also given for comparison.

| Country Name | 1966 | 1976 | 1986 | 1996 | 2006 | 2016 |
|---|---|---|---|---|---|---|
| Argentina | 6121 | 7292 | 6959 | 7955 | 9112 | 10149 |
| Australia | 21795 | 27827 | 32708 | 39066 | 49419 | 55671 |
| Bangladesh | 399 | 338 | 384 | 456 | 630 | 1030 |
| Brazil | 3746 | 7288 | 8315 | 8598 | 9762 | 10826 |
| Cameroon | 942 | 970 | 1727 | 1031 | 1180 | 1357 |
| Canada | 22242 | 29128 | 34737 | 37766 | 48035 | 50232 |
| China | 202 | 263 | 578 | 1335 | 3069 | 6894 |
| France | 16764 | 24175 | 28934 | 34497 | 40988 | 42013 |
| Greece | 10242 | 17500 | 18742 | 20389 | 29176 | 22736 |
| India | 318 | 373 | 458 | 657 | 1045 | 1861 |
| Indonesia | 666 | 989 | 1438 | 2358 | 2622 | 3974 |
| Italy | 14185 | 21341 | 27261 | 33243 | 37872 | 34284 |
| Japan | 13809 | 22147 | 31062 | 41515 | 44996 | 47608 |
| Kenya | 599 | 785 | 870 | 871 | 900 | 1143 |
| Korea, Rep. | 1278 | 2963 | 5953 | 12848 | 19427 | 25459 |
| Malaysia | 1765 | 2719 | 3701 | 6730 | 8274 | 11028 |
| Mexico | 4621 | 6127 | 6952 | 7604 | 9108 | 9707 |
| Netherlands | 20240 | 28385 | 31739 | 39626 | 49720 | 52111 |
| Pakistan | 397 | 491 | 667 | 834 | 1014 | 1182 |
| Philippines | 1177 | 1527 | 1390 | 1559 | 1880 | 2753 |
| Singapore | 4223 | 9959 | 16569 | 29951 | 42224 | 52601 |
| South Africa | 5508 | 6393 | 6086 | 5750 | 7055 | 7504 |
| Spain | 11229 | 16959 | 18752 | 24219 | 31865 | 31450 |
| Sweden | 22853 | 29722 | 34989 | 38198 | 52046 | 56319 |
| Thailand | 750 | 1142 | 1727 | 3689 | 4525 | 5901 |
| Turkey | 3863 | 5362 | 5936 | 7731 | 10251 | 14071 |
| United Kingdom | 15831 | 20126 | 25109 | 31300 | 40185 | 41603 |
| United States | 21274 | 26348 | 33134 | 39682 | 49575 | 52195 |
| Zimbabwe | 888 | 1241 | 1174 | 1312 | 769 | 909 |
| World | 4550 | 5847 | 6630 | 7525 | 9178 | 10391 |

Source: The World Bank: GDP per capita (constant 2010 US$): https://data.worldbank.org/indicator/NY.GDP.PCAP.KD

# Health data

The following table shows the prevalence of obesity among adults in different countries, in 1976, 1996 and 2016. Obesity is defined as BMI (Body Mass Index) greater than 30. The combined figure for both sexes is shown, together with figures for males and females.

|  | 1976 | | | 1996 | | | 2016 | | |
|---|---|---|---|---|---|---|---|---|---|
| Country name | Both sexes | Male | Female | Both sexes | Male | Female | Both sexes | Male | Female |
| Argentina | 11.5 | 9.3 | 13.5 | 19.1 | 17.3 | 20.6 | 28.3 | 27.3 | 29.0 |
| Australia | 10.8 | 10.0 | 11.5 | 18.1 | 17.7 | 18.5 | 29.0 | 29.6 | 28.4 |
| Bangladesh | 0.2 | 0.1 | 0.4 | 1.0 | 0.5 | 1.6 | 3.6 | 2.3 | 5.0 |
| Brazil | 5.5 | 3.2 | 7.6 | 12.7 | 9.3 | 15.8 | 22.1 | 18.5 | 25.4 |
| Cameroon | 1.4 | 0.5 | 2.3 | 4.8 | 2.0 | 7.4 | 11.4 | 6.1 | 16.4 |
| Canada | 10.1 | 9.1 | 11.0 | 18.2 | 17.5 | 18.8 | 29.4 | 29.5 | 29.3 |
| China | 0.5 | 0.2 | 0.8 | 1.8 | 1.3 | 2.4 | 6.2 | 5.9 | 6.5 |
| France | 9.1 | 7.0 | 10.9 | 14.5 | 13.2 | 15.6 | 21.6 | 22.0 | 21.1 |
| Greece | 10.2 | 7.1 | 12.9 | 17.1 | 14.4 | 19.6 | 24.9 | 24.2 | 25.4 |
| India | 0.4 | 0.2 | 0.6 | 1.3 | 0.7 | 1.9 | 3.9 | 2.7 | 5.1 |
| Indonesia | 0.5 | 0.2 | 0.7 | 1.9 | 0.9 | 2.9 | 6.9 | 4.8 | 8.9 |
| Italy | 8.6 | 6.6 | 10.3 | 13.8 | 12.5 | 14.9 | 19.9 | 20.1 | 19.5 |
| Japan | 1.1 | 0.7 | 1.5 | 1.8 | 1.5 | 2.1 | 4.3 | 4.8 | 3.7 |
| Kenya | 0.9 | 0.3 | 1.5 | 2.6 | 0.9 | 4.3 | 7.1 | 2.8 | 11.1 |
| Korea, Rep. | 1.8 | 0.9 | 2.5 | 3.6 | 2.5 | 4.4 | 6.8 | 6.1 | 7.3 |
| Malaysia | 1.5 | 0.7 | 2.4 | 5.5 | 3.5 | 7.5 | 15.6 | 13.0 | 17.9 |
| Mexico | 9.9 | 6.0 | 13.4 | 18.9 | 14.2 | 23.0 | 28.9 | 24.3 | 32.8 |
| Netherlands | 5.7 | 4.3 | 6.8 | 11.3 | 10.1 | 12.3 | 20.4 | 20.8 | 20.0 |
| Pakistan | 1.0 | 0.5 | 1.6 | 3.2 | 1.9 | 4.6 | 8.6 | 6.0 | 11.3 |
| Philippines | 0.7 | 0.4 | 1.1 | 2.7 | 1.8 | 3.6 | 6.4 | 5.2 | 7.5 |
| Singapore | 3.0 | 1.6 | 4.5 | 4.1 | 3.0 | 5.1 | 6.1 | 5.8 | 6.3 |
| South Africa | 10.2 | 2.4 | 17.5 | 17.6 | 6.2 | 27.8 | 28.3 | 15.4 | 39.6 |
| Spain | 10.1 | 7.9 | 11.8 | 17.0 | 15.6 | 18.1 | 23.8 | 24.6 | 22.8 |
| Sweden | 8.2 | 7.2 | 9.0 | 13.2 | 13.5 | 12.8 | 20.6 | 23.1 | 18.1 |
| Thailand | 0.9 | 0.4 | 1.4 | 3.0 | 1.5 | 4.4 | 10.0 | 7.0 | 12.7 |
| Turkey | 8.9 | 4.2 | 13.4 | 20.0 | 12.4 | 26.8 | 32.1 | 24.4 | 39.2 |
| United Kingdom | 9.6 | 8.1 | 11.0 | 16.6 | 15.0 | 18.2 | 27.8 | 26.9 | 28.6 |
| United States | 12.2 | 10.7 | 13.6 | 22.6 | 21.0 | 24.1 | 36.2 | 35.5 | 37.0 |
| Zimbabwe | 3.9 | 0.5 | 7.0 | 12.5 | 3.2 | 20.9 | 9.2 | 1.9 | 16.0 |

Source: WHO © 2016, Prevalence of obesity among adults, BMI ⩾ 30, age-standardized estimates by country http://apps.who.int/gho/data/node.main.A900A?lang=en (accessed 27 December, 2017).

# Health data (cont'd)

The following text gives details about obesity and related health conditions (e.g. diabetes).

**The problem of obesity**
In many countries, obesity, particularly childhood obesity, is a growing concern. Some of the contributors to this situation include sedentary lifestyles and consuming more processed foods and less fruits and vegetables. Even young children who are obese can face health concerns. Obesity can lead to serious diseases, such as type 2 diabetes, colon and breast cancers, and cardiovascular disease.

**How does the food consumed contribute to obesity?**
Fatty foods are calorie-dense. One gram of carbohydrates has four calories, one gram of protein has four calories, and one gram of fat has nine calories. Animals tend to seek fat-rich food for their higher energy content. Excess carbohydrate is used by the liver to synthesize glycogen. When there is more in the body than required, the resulting excess is converted into fatty acids. These are stored in adipose cells—the body's fat cells.

**How common is diabetes in the USA?**
Diabetes has been diagnosed in more than 18 million adults in the United States, and more than 200,000 children. It is estimated that up to 7 million more adults have the condition but have not been diagnosed. In addition, approximately 79 million people in the US are estimated to have pre-diabetes, a condition in which blood glucose levels are abnormally high, but not yet high enough to be classified as diabetes. For comparison, the population of the USA in 2017 was 326 million.

**Types of diabetes**
There are two main forms of diabetes. Type 1 is an autoimmune disease affecting the beta cells of the pancreas. This form of diabetes accounts for less than five percent of all diabetes cases. Type 2 diabetes accounts for approximately 95 percent of all cases. It is acquired, and lifestyle factors such as poor diet, inactivity, and the presence of pre-diabetes greatly increase a person's risk. About 80 to 90 percent of people with type 2 diabetes are overweight or obese. In many cases, type 2 diabetes can be reversed by moderate weight loss, regular physical activity, and consumption of a healthy diet; however, if blood glucose levels cannot be controlled, the diabetic will eventually require insulin.

**Risks from diabetes**
Over time, persistently high levels of glucose in the blood injure tissues, especially those of the blood vessels and nerves. Inflammation and injury of the arteries lead to atherosclerosis and an increased risk of heart attack and stroke. Damage to the blood vessels of the kidney impairs function and can lead to kidney failure. Damage to blood vessels that serve the eyes can lead to blindness. Together, these complications make diabetes the seventh leading cause of death in the United States.

*Sources: Adapted from Biology, Chapter 34: Animal Nutrition and the Digestive System © 2017 Rice University. Download for free at Download for free at https://openstax.org/details/books/biology*
*And Anatomy and Physiology, Chapter 17: The Endocrine System © 2017 Rice University. Download for free at Download for free at https://openstax.org/details/books/anatomy-and-physiology.*

# Sociology data

The following table gives data on **fertility** rates, **mortality** rates and net **migration** rates (all per 1,000 persons in the population, July 2017 estimates), together with **total population** figures for 2017. Population figures for 2000 are also given (to show growth).

| Country name | 2017 Fertility Rate | 2017 Mortality Rate | 2017 Migration Rate | 2017 Population | 2000 Population |
| --- | --- | --- | --- | --- | --- |
| Argentina | 16.7 | 7.5 | -0.1 | 44,293,293 | 36,955,182 |
| Australia | 12.1 | 7.3 | 5.5 | 23,232,413 | 19,169,083 |
| Bangladesh | 18.8 | 5.4 | -3.1 | 157,826,578 | 129,194,224 |
| Brazil | 14.1 | 6.7 | -0.1 | 207,353,391 | 172,860,370 |
| Cameroon | 35.4 | 9.6 | -0.1 | 24,994,885 | 15,421,937 |
| Canada | 10.3 | 8.7 | 5.7 | 35,623,680 | 31,281,092 |
| China | 12.3 | 7.8 | -0.4 | 1,379,302,771 | 1,261,832,482 |
| France | 12.2 | 9.3 | 1.1 | 67,106,161 | 59,329,691 |
| Greece | 8.4 | 11.3 | 2.3 | 10,768,477 | 10,601,527 |
| India | 19.0 | 7.3 | 0 | 1,281,935,911 | 1,014,003,817 |
| Indonesia | 16.2 | 6.5 | -1.1 | 260,580,739 | 224,784,210 |
| Italy | 8.6 | 10.4 | 3.7 | 62,137,802 | 57,634,327 |
| Japan | 7.7 | 9.8 | 0 | 126,451,398 | 126,549,976 |
| Kenya | 23.9 | 6.7 | -0.2 | 47,615,739 | 30,339,770 |
| Korea, Rep. | 8.3 | 6 | 2.5 | 51,181,299 | 47,470,969 |
| Malaysia | 19.1 | 5.1 | -0.3 | 31,381,992 | 21,793,293 |
| Mexico | 18.3 | 5.3 | -1.8 | 124,574,795 | 100,349,766 |
| Netherlands | 10.9 | 8.9 | 1.9 | 17,084,719 | 15,892,237 |
| Pakistan | 21.9 | 6.3 | -1.3 | 204,924,861 | 141,553,775 |
| Philippines | 23.7 | 6.1 | -2.0 | 104,256,076 | 81,159,644 |
| Singapore | 8.6 | 3.5 | 13.1 | 5,888,926 | 4,151,264 |
| South Africa | 20.2 | 9.4 | -0.9 | 54,841,552 | 43,421,021 |
| Spain | 9.2 | 9.1 | 7.8 | 48,958,159 | 39,996,671 |
| Sweden | 12.1 | 9.4 | 5.3 | 9,960,487 | 8,873,052 |
| Thailand | 11.0 | 8.0 | 0 | 68,414,135 | 61,230,874 |
| Turkey | 15.7 | 6.0 | -4.5 | 80,845,215 | 65,666,677 |
| United Kingdom | 12.1 | 9.4 | 2.5 | 64,769,452 | 59,511,464 |
| United States | 12.5 | 8.2 | 3.9 | 326,625,791 | 275,562,673 |
| Zimbabwe | 34.2 | 10.2 | -8.5 | 13,805,084 | 11,342,521 |

The World Factbook 2017. Washington, DC: Central Intelligence Agency, 2017, https://www.cia.gov/library/publications/the-world-factbook/index.html (accessed 27 December, 2017).

# Sociology data (cont'd)

The following text gives information on demography and population.

**Demography and Population**
Between 2011 and 2012, we reached a population milestone of 7 billion humans on the earth's surface. The rapidity with which this happened demonstrated an exponential increase from the time it took to grow from 5 billion to 6 billion people. In short, the planet is filling up. How quickly will we go from 7 billion to 8 billion? How will that population be distributed? Where is population the highest? Where is it slowing down? Where will people live? To explore these questions, we turn to **demography**, or the study of populations. Three of the most important components that affect the issues above are fertility, mortality, and migration.

The **fertility** rate of a society is a measure noting the number of children born. Sociologists measure fertility using the crude birth rate (the number of live births per 1,000 people per year). Just as fertility measures childbearing, the **mortality** rate is a measure of the number of people who die. The crude death rate is a number derived from the number of deaths per 1,000 people per year. When analyzed together, fertility and mortality rates help researchers understand the overall growth occurring in a population.

Another key element in studying populations is **migration**, the movement of people into and out of an area. Migration may take the form of immigration, which describes movement into an area to take up permanent residence, or emigration, which refers to movement out of an area to another place of permanent residence. Migration might be voluntary (as when college students study abroad), involuntary (as when Syrians evacuated war-torn areas), or forced (as when many Native American tribes were removed from the lands they had lived in for generations).

Changing fertility, mortality, and migration rates make up the total population composition, a snapshot of the demographic profile of a population. This number can be measured for societies, nations, world regions, or other groups. The population composition includes the sex ratio, the number of men for every hundred women, as well as the population pyramid, a picture of population distribution by sex and age.

*Source: Adapted from Introduction to Sociology, 2nd Edition, Chapter 20: Population, Urbanization, and the Environment © 2017 Rice University. Download for free at Download for free at Download for free at https://openstax.org/details/books/introduction-sociology-2e.*

# Appendix 5: Presentation planning grid

Use this grid to help you plan the main points of your presentation and the language.

Hook: _____
_____

Topic/focus: _____
_____

Purpose: _____
_____

Structure

1. _____

2. _____

3. _____

Timing: _____ minutes

---

1st main point: _____

Details

_____
_____
_____
_____
_____

---

**Arouse interest ('hook')**
- Let me ask you a question…

**Greet the audience/Introduce yourself**
- Good morning/afternoon everyone. My name is…

**State the topic/focus**
- What I want to talk about today is…
- What I'm going to look at today is…

**Expressing the purpose**
- My purpose/objective/aim today is…
- What I want to do this morning/afternoon/today is…

**Giving the structure**
- This talk is divided into 3 main parts.
- To start with/Firstly, I'd like to look at…
- Then/Secondly, I'll be talking about…
- Finally, I'll be looking at…

**Giving the timing**
- My presentation/talk/lecture will take/last about 10/15/20 minutes.

**Handling questions**
- At the end of my talk, there will be a chance to ask questions.
- If you have any questions, I'll be happy to answer them at the end.

**Transitions**
- Let's now move on to/turn to…
- I now want to go on to…
- This leads/brings me to my next point, which is…
- I'd now like to move on to/turn to…
- So far we have looked at… Now I'd like to…

# Appendices

**2nd main point:** _____

**Details**

_____

_____

_____

_____

_____

_____

**Transitions**
- Let's now move on to/turn to...
- I now want to go on to...
- This leads/brings me to my next point, which is...
- I'd now like to move on to/turn to...
- So far we have looked at... Now I'd like to...

**3rd main point:** _____

**Details**

_____

_____

_____

_____

_____

_____

**Transitions**
- Let's now move on to/turn to...
- I now want to go on to...
- This leads/brings me to my next point, which is...
- I'd now like to move on to/turn to...
- So far we have looked at... Now I'd like to...

**Summing up**
- To summarise...
- So, to sum up...
- To recap...
- Let me now sum up.

**Concluding (take-away message)**
- Let me end by saying...
- I'd like to finish by emphasising...
- In conclusion I'd like to say...

**Closing**
- Thank you for your attention.

**Questions**
- If you have any questions, I'll be happy to answer them now.
- If there are any questions, I'll do my best to answer them.

**Summary**

1. _____

2. _____

3. _____

**Conclusion:** _____

_____

_____

# Appendix 6: **Presentation outline**

The following presentation outline can be used to practise *language* (Unit 3), *body language* (Unit 5) and *delivery* (Unit 6). It is useful if you do not have – or have not finished – a presentation of your own. Some exercises in each of the above units require that you have a presentation to work with. This outline is on the topic of *Learning Styles*, and the full introduction can be found in the exercise section of Unit 2 and Unit 6. Note that *this is only an outline*. As such, it is quite brief and uses outline format, with symbols and abbreviations.

<u>Learning Styles</u>

<u>Introduction</u>
- Arouse interest
    - Qu: How do you prefer to learn? E.g. group/on own, listen/see, snack, music, etc.
    - Differences in how we learn = 'learning styles' (definition)
    - Understanding yours is important 1st step in improving study
- Greet audience
- Introduce self
- State topic: learning styles
- State focus: two of the main models of learning style used in educational contexts
- Give outline:
    1) historical overview of learning styles
    2) details of two main models: VAK, Dunn and Dunn
    3) ways learning styles can improve study
- State aim: think about your learning style and how to use it to improve learning
- Give timing
- Inform about handling questions

<u>1) Historical overview</u>
- Educators first interested in learning styles in the mid-1970s
- Cause: Kolb's learning cycle
    - this has four stages, which all learners pass through (plan, do reflect, conclude)
    - Kolb suggested that learners prefer some aspects of the cycle to others
    - Kolb identified four learning styles related to his learning cycle
    - his styles were not based on research
- Many more theories since then
- Some studies suggest over 70 different models!

2) Two main models
- VAK model
    - Perhaps the most well-known model
    - VAK is short for Visual, Auditory, and Kinaesthetic (three styles)
    - Visual learners:
        - learn best by seeing
        - e.g. pictures, handouts, charts, graphs, maps, visual aids, colour-coding, reading
    - Auditory learners:
        - learn best by listening
        - e.g. lectures, recordings, discussions, debates, repeating words
    - Kinaesthetic learners:
        - learn best by moving and touching
        - e.g. physical movement, projects, experiments, field trips, frequent breaks
- Dunn and Dunn model
    - Widely used in USA
    - Describes individuals' reactions to 21 different elements, such as sound, light, motivation, individual work
    - Elements are grouped under five dimensions: environmental, emotional, sociological, physiological, and psychological.
    - Leads to questions such as the following:
        - Does the learner like to study in a cool or warm environment?
        - Does the learner need a lot of emotional support and encouragement?
        - Does the learner prefer to work alone or with others?
        - Does the learner like to snack while learning?
        - When does the learner learn best? Morning? Midday? Evening?

3) How learning styles can improve learning
- First, be aware of different learning styles
    - everyone has different preferences, including how they learn
    - if possible, find out about some other popular models (e.g. Kolb, Honey and Mumford)
- Second, try identify your style
    - perhaps try online questionnaires to help you to identify your own style
    - may depend on which model you think is most convincing (VAK? Dunn and Dunn?)
- Finally, try to adapt your study to take your preferred styles into account, e.g.:
    - use more images and pictures if you are a visual learner, recordings if auditory
    - work with others if it helps, think about best time of day

Conclusion
- Summary
- 'Take-away' message: No right or wrong style, understanding yours may improve learning
- Thank audience
- Invite questions